Mystery of the Magi

in the Bible never happened at all. Dwight Longenecker's *Mystery of the Magi* is the perfect Christmas gift for anyone interested in the historical background behind the birth of Jesus of Nazareth and what his birth means for us today. I highly recommend this wonderful book."

—**Robert J. Hutchinson**, author of *The Politically Incorrect Guide® to the Bible, The Dawn of Christianity*, and *Searching for Jesus*

"Dwight Longenecker's *Mystery of the Magi* is a fascinating and thought-provoking contribution to a topic either saddled with fanciful stories or subjected to harsh revisionism. His study is both detailed and academic, while honestly asking important questions about the true identity and meaning of the wise men and their quest."

—**Dr. Matthew Bunson**, senior contributor at Eternal Word Television Network

"In this beautifully written and important book Dwight Longenecker provides a fascinating new solution to the questions 'Who were the Magi who visited Jesus and where did they come from?' The book is aimed at readers with no prior knowledge of the Bible and also at biblical scholars. I believe it succeeds admirably for both audiences. In addition, it is a mine of useful information about the Middle East at the time of Christ. It is the best book I know about the Magi and throws new light upon the birth narratives in the gospels. Buy it as a present for others or for yourself!"

—**Sir Colin John Humphreys, Ph.D.**, professor and director of research at the University of Cambridge and author of *The Mystery of the Last Supper*

"The story of the Magi in Matthew's Gospel has fascinated historians for centuries. It has also been the subject of much speculation by theologians and elaboration by artists. Dwight Longenecker presents an extremely readable account of the problems and tackles the issue of the identity of the Magi in a novel way—by seeking to locate their place of origin in northwest Arabia. Dwight Longenecker has written a wonderful book. It is a refreshing account which will enrich the reader's appreciation of the gospel tradition."

—**John Healey, Ph.D.**, professor emeritus at the University of Manchester and fellow of the British Academy

"Over time, the historical account of the Magi was overgrown by legendary mythologies, the way a wall might be overgrown by ivy. Fr. Longenecker can appreciate that flowering of tradition, but wants to know if we can still find the bricks beneath. He proposes we can and unfolds this investigation of the historical Magi with clarity and ease, in a way that will fascinate the reader."

—**David W. Fagerberg, Ph.D.**, professor at the University of Notre Dame

"The wise men who visited the infant Jesus are among the most mysterious figures in history. Here Dwight Longenecker discovers little-known clues and pieces them together, weaving a detective story that unravels the mystery of just who the Magi were. Highly intriguing reading for Bible students, history buffs, and lovers of mystery!"

—**Jimmy Akin**, senior apologist for Catholic Answers

"It is difficult to put this book down without being persuaded of the historicity of Saint Matthew's account of the story of the Magi. Much of this is due to Dwight Longenecker's insightful, diligent, and lively sleuth work on a great mass of scholarly research into the history and traditions of the people of the Ancient Near East, especially those who claimed Abrahamic heritage. The result is an illumination of the importance of all scriptural details about Abraham's descendants, of the representative importance of their hopes, and of the astonishing way in which the gospel shows Providence to have fulfilled and transcended

those hopes. This is vital reading for all who love and wish to understand Scripture more deeply—scholars included."
—**Gregory Y. Glazov, Ph.D.**, professor at Seton Hall University's Immaculate Conception Seminary School of Theology

"If a skeptic wants to ridicule the Christmas story, there is no better place to start than with the story of the Magi who come to worship the Christ child. To be sure, all kinds of legends have attached themselves to the simple account in Matthew 2. But if one sticks to the biblical story and is willing to dig deeply into ancient history, a plausible account of courtiers of a nearby Nabatean king, generally on friendly terms with King Herod, emerges. Longenecker does more than this, however: he discusses the origins of Matthew's gospel, Paul's three years in Arabia, and the convergence of Essenes, Nabateans, magi, and Paul in Damascus, in a veritable detective story. If not every detail is equally convincing, every section of the investigation is equally fascinating. This book deserves serious scrutiny."
—**Craig L. Blomberg, Ph.D.**, distinguished professor at Denver Seminary and author of *The Historical Reliability of the Gospels*

"In this fascinating, carefully researched, and well-written book, Dwight Longenecker steers a careful course between the pitfalls of unreflective piety that accepts all the legends that have grown up and smothered the wise men and the quicksand of impious scholarship that sees them as nothing more than mere myths of Matthew's imagination. Longenecker uncovers and presents an explanation of the Magi that is faithful to both history and Matthew's story. Basic believers and critical scholars will find themselves encouraged and enlightened by this fresh look at one of the Christian faith's most enduring stories."
—**Dr. Leroy A. Huizenga, Ph.D.**, administrative chair at the University of Mary

"Fr. Longenecker's *Mystery of the Magi* reads like a good whodunit as he traces the various attempts to identify the Magi who visited Jesus. As readers tread the path the author lays out, they are educated in a fashion they might not have expected. En route, they learn much about the Christian traditions of the Magi. Two results stand out. We see how groundless is modern scholars' rejection of the historicity of the original event, rejection borne of misguided skepticism. Fr. Longenecker's book also beckons us to delve more into the Church Fathers' handling of the Magi and the lessons to be gleaned from them."

　　—**Kenneth J. Howell**, president of the Pontifical
　　　　Studies Foundation and academic director of the
　　　　Eucharist Project

"The Magi of Matthew's gospel are enigmatic figures. Later Christian imagination transformed them into philosophers, kings, or even fictitious characters who showed that prophecies had been fulfilled. Longenecker believes they were historical figures, wise teachers from the kingdom of Nabataea, who had preserved in Petra the prophecies and wisdom of old Jerusalem.

"This book is packed with fascinating information: where Isaiah's disciples fled during the exile and preserved his teachings, the origin of the mysterious Nabateans and their links to Babylon, the politics of the Herodian kings, the fact that Herod the Great was the son of a Nabatean princess, theories about the star of Bethlehem, and why Saint Paul went to Arabia after his conversion experience.

"Longenecker's Magi are no longer exotic kings from distant lands; they are real figures, the pieces missing from many ancient puzzles."

　　—**Dr. Margaret Barker**, former president of the Society
　　　　for Old Testament Study and co-founder of the Temple
　　　　Studies Group

"Fr. Longenecker's impressive and deeply researched *Mystery of the Magi* is part history lesson, part detective story, and part theological reflection. It demonstrates, in many ways, how and why Christianity is rooted in history and, thus, not only doesn't fear the truth but also joyfully pursues it. As Fr. Longenecker rightly says about the story of the Magi, 'This matters because history matters, and history matters because truth matters.'"

—**Carl E. Olson**, editor of the *Catholic World Report* and author of *Did Jesus Really Rise from the Dead?*

"Fr. Longenecker begins with the startling (to some) assumption that the Scriptures are accurate when they describe the Magi seeking the Christ Child. He then proceeds to sift the wheat of revelation from the chaff of legend, sentiment, and cultural accretion, taking the reader on a wide-ranging survey of the historical setting of the Nativity. He explores the sources of some of the legends and navigates through modern trends in Scriptural exegesis to bring forth a scholarly yet accessible work regarding who the Magi were, where they came from, and what they were looking for. This book is both engaging and informative."

—**Roger Thomas**, author of *From Afar* and *The Accidental Marriage*

MYSTERY
OF THE
Magi

THE QUEST TO IDENTIFY THE THREE WISE MEN

DWIGHT LONGENECKER

REGNERY
HISTORY

Regnery History™ is a trademark of Salem Communications Holding Corporation; Regnery® is a registered trademark and its colophon is a trademark of Salem Communications Holding Corporation

Cataloging-in-Publication data on file with the Library of Congress

First trade paperback edition published 2021

ISBN: 978-1-68451-257-7

Published in the United States by
Regnery History
An Imprint of Regnery Publishing
A Division of Salem Media Group
Washington, D.C.
www.RegneryHistory.com

Manufactured in the United States of America

10 9 8 7 6 5 4 3 2 1

Books are available in quantity for promotional or premium use. For information on discounts and terms, please visit our website: www.Regnery.com.

To Richard Ballard—a wise man

PROPOSED
Routes of the Magi

▬▬▬	Magi Route to Jerusalem and Bethlehem
═══	Magi Route away from Bethlehem
••••••	Mary and Joseph's Route to Bethlehem
– – –	Other Trade Routes

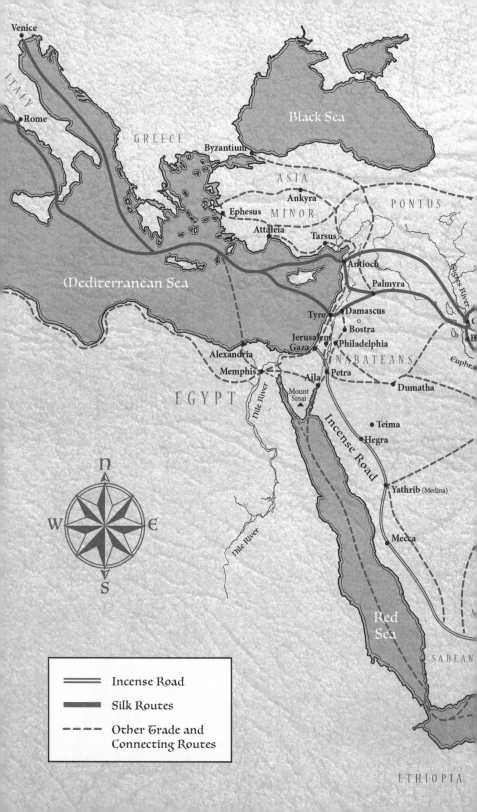

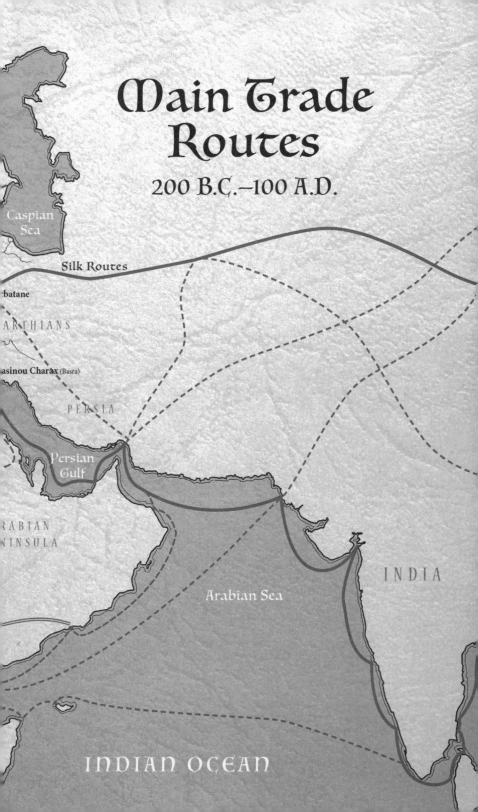

CONTENTS

The Three Wise Men: Facts or Fairy Tale?

It's the night of the Christmas play, and everyone has arrived in his holiday best. The parents and teachers have set out cookies and festive punch. The children are in their costumes backstage, breathless with excitement. The fifth-graders, in bathrobes, are shepherds, their heads covered with towels tied round with cord, while the second-graders are angels this year—gowns made up quickly from old sheets, tinsel halos, and glitter-sprinkled cardboard wings strapped to their backs.

The kindergarten kids are wearing donkey ears, and the first-graders are Victorian carolers. Mary is pretty in blue, and sixth-grade Joseph looks solemn in his over-the-ears beard. He's nervous because he has to put his arm around Mary, and the other boys are going to laugh at him.

Behind them, ready to follow the star to Bethlehem, are the three wise sixth-graders, resplendent in purple, scarlet, and gold satin robes. One boy is from a Syrian refugee family. Another is from India. The third is African American. Wearing a turban and crown, each one carries an ornate little casket. One with gold. One with frankincense. One with myrrh.

We can all visualize the scene. It's part of the magic of Christmas, along with a whole collection of enchanting traditions that have accumulated over centuries. The school Christmas play, the Nativity scene, Christmas cards, carols by candlelight, "O Little Town of Bethlehem," the tree, the gifts, the feasts, and family visits.

In the midst of secular Christmas, with Frosty the Snowman and Santa, Rudolph the Red-Nosed Reindeer and Bing Crosby dreaming of a white Christmas, we want the wonderful story of the Christ child born in a stable, heralded by angels, honored by shepherds, and worshipped by kings who followed a star.

Even the most hardened cynics want to keep Christmas. Despite the rise of casual unbelief, most of us want to hand the family Nativity set on to our children. Hypocrites and agnostics, we still gather for church at that one time each year. It may be far from our everyday lives, and we may not really believe, but many of us *want* to believe. Even if we don't, we want to hear again the story of the innocent mother and the faithful father. Even if we have doubts, we want to hear about the angels singing to the shepherds and the sweet old story of the wise men who were enchanted by a miraculous star.

But is there any truth to it all?

Christmas Secular and Sacred

For most of us, the stories and customs of Christmas are bundled up like presents under the tree. They all have the same colorful wrapping, glitter, and appeal, but the contents vary. One box might hold a priceless treasure from a dear friend, while another might be a cheap trinket bought out of a sense of duty by someone who couldn't care less. Some presents are given to impress, others to make us laugh, still others to be treasured forever.

When it comes to the Christmas stories, the historical and factual are mixed with the magical and mysterious. Some stories and customs are modern and easily understood. Others are ancient, and their origins have been lost over the span of centuries. We might realize that "The Night Before Christmas" is an American poem from the nineteenth century, but who knows what "wassail" is?

We deck the halls with boughs of holly and decorate the Christmas tree, but how many of us know these are originally pagan traditions from Germany? "Rudolph the Red-Nosed Reindeer" is a commercial spin-off from Santa's flying sleigh, but do you know why there are "twelve drummers drumming" or "ten lords a-leaping"? You recognize Santa Claus as "jolly old Saint Nick," a twinkly-eyed grandpa, but did you know Saint Nicholas was a feisty, fourth-century bishop from Turkey who was not associated with Christmas until many centuries after his death?

The Christmas story has been cluttered up with so many customs, traditions, legends, and strange characters over the years that it's difficult to imagine that any of it might be rooted in history. We've heard the story of Mary and Joseph traveling to Bethlehem. We know about the grumpy innkeeper, the stable, the ox, the ass, and the manger bed. We know about angels singing to shepherds and the three kings who followed the star, but in our minds we bundle those stories up with flying reindeer, singing snowmen, Santa Claus, and a collection of heart-warming Christmas movies that always feature pretty snowstorms, Christmas trees, and the welcome of family, hearth, and home.

It's a sentimental season glowing with gift-giving, goodwill, and "God bless us, every one!" So is it worth trying to sift through the fantastic fairy tales and lovely legends to discover the truth behind the tinsel, or is it easier just to light the candles, sing the carols, and keep it all in the great big box of magical make-believe?

King Arthur and Santa

The fact of the matter is that facts matter. If an event is historical, it is real, and if it is real, then it affects the rest of history. If an event really happened, we have to pay attention and fit it into our vision of reality. If we regard the Bible stories as fairy tales but then learn that they are historical, we are compelled to reconsider our understanding of history and the other claims of Christianity.

The problem is that when we are dealing with ancient stories, separating fact from fiction is rarely easy. History and fantasy get jumbled up together. A good example is King Arthur. Historians believe there probably was a real chieftain named Arthur who ruled some British tribes during the time of the Saxon invasions. Who Arthur was, however, and how he lived and where Camelot was located are difficult to ascertain. Furthermore, the historical Arthur is a far cry from the character in Malory's *Le Morte d'Arthur*, Tennyson's *Idylls of the King*, and T. H. White's *The Once and Future King*—not to mention Disney's animated *Sword in the Stone* or *Monty Python and the Holy Grail*.

In a similar way, in most historical accounts of the ancient world there are kernels of fact beneath the fanciful tales. Over the years the much-loved stories are shared and elaborated. They evolve with time and the telling. People move and take their stories with them. New cultures interact with old, and the stories develop and change. It is the work of scholars to dig deep and find the foundation of truth that lies beneath the legend.

Another good example of how this happens is the story of Santa Claus. We view Santa as the man in a red and white costume at the shopping mall who chortles "Ho! Ho! Ho!," poses for pictures, and gives the kids a candy cane. But where did Santa Claus come from?

The name is derived from Sinterklaas, the old Dutch name for Saint Nicholas. When the Dutch settled in New Amsterdam, "Sinterklaas" became "Sancta Klaus," which was eventually shortened to "Santa Claus."

Saint Nicholas was the bishop of Myra in Asia Minor (modern Turkey). Famous for his compassion for needy children, he became the patron saint of children, and his memorial day of December 6 was celebrated with various charming traditions across Europe. The Dutch portrayed "Sinterklaas" as an old man with a long, white beard and a bishop's pointed hat, staff, and red robes who rode on a white horse across the rooftops dropping gifts for children down their chimneys.

Meanwhile, in Puritan England in the seventeenth century, the Catholic Saint Nicholas developed into the nonreligious Father Christmas. When John Leech illustrated Charles Dickens's *A Christmas Carol*, he portrayed the Ghost of Christmas Present as a jolly and generous old man wearing an English-style green cloak with holly in his hair. Two decades later, in 1863, the American illustrator Thomas Nast portrayed Saint Nicholas as a rotund, bearded figure, his bishop's robes now replaced by a warm, red winter outfit. By the 1930s Santa had fully evolved into the red-and-white-suited, oversized guzzler of Coca-Cola who has ridden the advertising waves to global fame.

The story of Saint Nicholas and Santa is a perfect example of how a historical figure can give rise to legends that, taking on a life of their own, eventually produce a mythical and magical figure. The same thing happened to those earlier mystical men of Christmas—the three wise men we call the Magi.

Believers with Blinders

The story of the Magi began with a simple account recorded in the second chapter of the gospel according to Matthew. It goes like this:

> After Jesus was born in Bethlehem in Judea, during the
> time of King Herod, Magi from the east came to Jerusalem

and asked, "Where is the one who has been born king of the Jews? We saw his star when it rose and have come to worship him."

When King Herod heard this he was disturbed, and all Jerusalem with him. When he had called together all the people's chief priests and teachers of the law, he asked them where the Messiah was to be born. "In Bethlehem in Judea," they replied, "for this is what the prophet has written:
"'But you, Bethlehem, in the land of Judah,
are by no means least among the rulers of Judah;
for out of you will come a ruler
who will shepherd my people Israel.'"

Then Herod called the Magi secretly and found out from them the exact time the star had appeared. He sent them to Bethlehem and said, "Go and search carefully for the child. As soon as you find him, report to me, so that I too may go and worship him."

After they had heard the king, they went on their way, and the star they had seen when it rose went ahead of them until it stopped over the place where the child was. When they saw the star, they were overjoyed. On coming to the house, they saw the child with his mother Mary, and they bowed down and worshiped him. Then they opened their treasures and presented him with gifts of gold, frankincense and myrrh. And having been warned in a dream not to go back to Herod, they returned to their country by another route.[1]

Anyone who reads Matthew's story closely will notice immediately that certain details we all take for granted are missing. There are no camels. The wise men are not named Caspar, Balthasar, and Melchior. And the text does not say that there are only three of them. Matthew doesn't even hint that the wise men are kings, and he doesn't say they came from Persia, India, China, or Africa. In fact, he doesn't say they came from far away. He simply says they were "from the East." Neither does the text say that they followed the star across the desert sands to Jerusalem. It simply says, "We saw his star when it rose."

Finally, the popular idea, reinforced by millions of crèches, that the wise men adored the child alongside the shepherds in the stable on Christmas night has no basis in Matthew's account. There are no shepherds when the Magi arrive in Bethlehem, and they find Mary and the child not in a stable but in a "house." Furthermore, we get the impression that the "child" is no longer a newborn.

Where did all the other beloved details come from? It is clear that very soon after Matthew's gospel was published, the story of the three wise men began to be elaborated on, and before long many details were added to Matthew's simple account.

Just as there are fascinating explanations for the evolution of the Saint Nicholas story, so there are intriguing explanations for how the extra details found their way into the Magi story. We'll answer those questions in chapter three, but first we have to ask whether the story is completely make-believe or whether there might be historical events lying beneath the story as we know it.

As soon as we ask that question, alarm bells go off among Christian believers. The elaborate version of the Christmas story has been part of their culture and faith for two thousand years. Because the old inspiring stories were learned in childhood, they are comforting, and because they are part of the ancient tradition, they make believers feel secure and safe. "This is the story as it's been told for thousands of years," the believers protest, "and this is how it always will be told!"

There is an even more important problem. Christians believe the Bible is the Word of God. If the Magi story isn't true, then perhaps the Bible is untrustworthy. If the story of the Magi is a fairy tale, then why wouldn't other, more important Bible stories also be fairy tales?

If we can't believe the story of the Magi, why should we believe the story of the Virgin Birth? And if we can't believe the story of the Virgin Birth, why should we believe in the resurrection of Jesus from the dead, and why should we believe he is the Son of God? You can see why Christian believers are upset by the suggestion that the story of the wise men is just a piece of magical make-believe.

Therefore they insist that the Magi story is historically true, and they pass the stories down to the next generation. In the glow of Christmas lights, the figures of Balthasar, Melchior, and Caspar are reverently placed in the Christmas stable, the sixth-graders process solemnly in the school play, the wise men present their gifts, the choir sings "We Three Kings of Orient Are," and the great legend continues.

Resisting the truth, too many believers want to stay in their religious "safe space." They prefer to believe the childish, sentimental version of the story of the exotic wise men, with all its delightful details, as someone might prefer Disney's *Pocahontas* to the historical facts. They are what I call "believers with blinders." They do not wish to see the truth—even if the truth might set them free.

Scholars and Skeptics

Meanwhile, the scholars and skeptics take the opposite position. They want to cut away all the accretions, to get down to the bare bones of the story and deliver modern believers from what they consider to be no more than myths and fairy tales. After studying the texts, many scholars come to the conclusion that the story of the three wise men is nothing more than a complicated patchwork of fanciful fiction, theological lessons, and pious legends.[2]

Furthermore, they think the story of exotic sages from a faraway land following a magical star to worship the Son of God is incredible in our modern, scientific age. Consequently, the majority of Biblical scholars dismiss the story of the Magi as an invention of the early

Christians to boost the claim that Jesus of Nazareth was the promised Messiah—the supernatural Son of God.[3]

Biblical scholars are not preachers. They are not necessarily Christian believers. Their task is the painstaking analysis of the ancient texts so that all of us can understand them better. Biblical scholars therefore approach the gospels with the tools proper to literary, historical, archaeological, and linguistic research, building on the results of over one hundred years of detailed Biblical scholarship. Like detectives, they sift through the Biblical texts and the other evidence in an attempt to discern what is historical in the stories and what is not.

The problem is that Biblical scholars often work under their own set of prejudices. Assuming that miracles are impossible, they conclude that the supernatural elements of the gospel stories must be imaginary additions. This bias infects everything they do. If the believers with blinders assume that everything in the Bible stories must be true, the scholars and skeptics too often assume that everything in the Bible is false.

In fact, the truth lies somewhere in the middle, and one of the exciting things about exploring the story of the Magi is that we can embark on a fascinating adventure of discovery. To do so we will take advantage of the strengths of both sides of the debate. Assuming, like the believers, that the Bible stories are essentially historical and trustworthy, we will use the tools of the scholars to examine the text, study the elaborations, cut away what is legendary, and learn more about the context and history of the New Testament times.

Step by step, like detectives solving a difficult case, we will gather and collate the evidence, analyze our findings, and think through all the possibilities to find the truth behind the mystery of the Magi. Who was Matthew, and when did he write his gospel? Could he have spoken to eyewitnesses of the events he describes? Could the wise men have been historical figures? If so, who were they? Where did they come from? What was their worldview? What were their political, economic, and cultural motivations? What did they believe, and why was it important for them to pay homage to a newborn king of the Jews?

Why did Matthew record the story? What did it mean to him? Why was it important to his audience? What about the elements in the story that seem supernatural? Could there be a natural explanation, or did someone fabricate the exotic magicians, the star, and the mystical dreams to make the story of Christ's birth more wonderful?

The results of this journey of discovery are astounding. They turn upside down the assumptions of both the believers in blinders and the scholars and skeptics. The explosive findings in this book will shake the comfortable worlds of the conservative Christians and "radical" skeptics. Theories and traditions that have reigned for more than a hundred years will be challenged, and a new understanding of the relationship of the New Testament to its time will unfold.

Be warned. What you discover on this journey will make you reassess your understanding of the life of Jesus of Nazareth, the reality of the Christian message, and your own comfortable worldview.

The adventure on which we are about to embark will be like the journey of the Magi itself. We will be required to set out from our comfort zone and launch into a quest—not knowing what our final destination will be. I promise you, the trek will be an adventure. We will have to work hard, take some wrong turns, and pick our way through a maze of information and data. Like the Magi, we may encounter hardships, doubt, confusion, and fear.

To complete the journey we will need curiosity, intelligence, perseverance, and, as in the Magi's own experience, it won't do any harm to look for some guidance from above.

CHAPTER ONE

Is the Bible True?

When most people say a story is "true," they mean "it really happened that way." Even though a story might be exaggerated or embellished, we say a story is true if it relates actual events.

However, we might also say that a story is "true" if it communicates truth. In that sense a fairy tale like "Cinderella," a fable like "The Tortoise and the Hare," a movie, or a novel might be "true" even though it is not historical.

But there is a third type of "true" story, one that is factually true and communicates greater truths. Here is an example. In December 1944 my grandfather was walking to the farmer's market in Pottstown, Pennsylvania, with his two young sons—aged ten and twelve. It was the week before Christmas. Snow was on the ground, and the roads were treacherous. As they crossed the bridge over the Schuylkill River they stepped carefully because its surface was icy. When they were halfway across, a fully loaded coal truck turned the corner and came onto the bridge. It hit an icy patch and careened toward the boys. My grandfather jumped to push the boys to safety but was hit by the truck, which crushed him against the guardrails.

When well-meaning bystanders folded his broken body into the back of a car to rush him to hospital, his splintered ribs punctured his internal organs, and he began to bleed internally. Two days later, he lay in a hospital bed with my grandmother by his side. As they were praying together, he opened his eyes and looked to the corner of the room. Suddenly, my grandmother recounted, his face was filled with radiance, and he said, "Can't you see them, my dear? Can't you see them? They are so beautiful!" Then he was gone.

This story is not only factually true but also deeply moving. It engages our emotions, communicating deep truths about a father's love for his sons, the beauty and heroism of self-sacrifice, the reality of heaven, and the possibility of a good, noble, and redemptive death.

Stories like this—true in both senses of the word—are called "testimony stories." They are the stories that are most precious to us. They are the most powerful stories, because the greater truths are wrapped up in events that really happened at a certain time and place to real people.

Dissecting the Gospels

For sixteen hundred years most Christians believed the stories told in the Bible were testimony stories. They believed the Bible stories not only communicated truth but also were historically true.

Then in the mid-seventeenth century, scholars began to question the accuracy of ancient texts. Thomas Hobbes (d. 1679), Benedict Spinoza (d. 1677), and others began to examine who wrote the books of the Bible, questioning their historical accuracy. They dissected the ancient documents with rational and logical tools. The fruit of their analysis was summed up by the Enlightenment scholar H. S. Reimarus (d. 1768), who concluded that very little in the stories about Jesus of Nazareth was historically reliable.

Doubts about the historical accuracy of the New Testament continued into the nineteenth century with the work of the Frenchman Ernest Renan (d. 1892) and, a generation later, imbued the young Albert Schweitzer's *Quest of the Historical Jesus* (1906). Books debating the true personality and message of Jesus are still being churned out today, as scholars continue to analyze the quest for the historical Jesus.[1]

The same technique was applied to other ancient writings. For example, *The Iliad*—the Greek epic about the Trojan War by the poet Homer—was considered to be nothing but a legend. Then, in the 1860s the amateur archaeologists Frank Calvert and Heinrich Schliemann announced that they had unearthed the ancient city of Troy on a hillside in Turkey, and the world of literary and historical scholarship was turned upside down. Scholars mocked Schliemann as an amateur, publicity-seeking adventurer. Eventually their work was taken seriously, however, and from Calvert and Schliemann's Indiana-Jones-type sleuthing the modern scientific approach to archaeology emerged.

A similar thing happened with the discovery in 1946 of the Dead Sea Scrolls. A shepherd boy found some ancient manuscripts in a cave, and suddenly a whole new perspective on the Scriptures and the religion and culture of ancient Palestine opened up. Subsequent advances in technology and forensics, as well as new disciplines like archaeo-astronomy, enable us to take a fresh look at the fascinating history of the ancient world.

At the same time, since the 1960s a new generation of scholars has made steady advances in the analysis of the New Testament. Theories about the dating of its books that once seemed watertight are proving to be leaky. Research continues, and new discoveries are revolutionizing our understanding of the ancient texts.

The Biblical scholar Margaret Barker comments on the revolutionary nature of recent research: "The impact of the last fifty years

of discoveries has been comparable to the impact of the Bible translations on the Reformation. New questions have been raised and old
certainties have been challenged."[2] The old certainties of both the
"believers with blinders" and the "scholars and skeptics" are being
re-examined, and as new information is uncovered the established
theories are being overturned.

Among these are the theories concerning the narratives of the
birth of Christ.

History or Mystery?

The familiar tales of Christmas are found in the gospels according to Luke and Matthew. Luke tells the story from Mary's point of
view, recounting the miraculous birth after she was visited by an
angel and supplying the familiar details of the journey to Bethlehem,
the search for lodging, the birth in the stable, the vision of angels,
and the visit of the shepherds.

Matthew tells the story from Joseph's point of view. An angel
reassures and guides Joseph not to reject Mary despite her scandalous
pregnancy. Matthew includes the visit of the Magi, the slaughter of
baby boys by King Herod, and Joseph's flight with Mary and the
child into Egypt before finally returning to settle in Nazareth.

We are going to focus on the story of the Magi, but before we can
discover who the wise men might have been, we have to ask whether
the Magi story has any foundation in history.

As the scholars dismissed the historical reality of Troy, so most
Bible scholars dismiss the narratives about the birth of Jesus Christ.
They propose that the stories of Jesus' birth were invented many years
after his crucifixion to bolster the Church's claims that he was the Son
of God.[3] Others say we should treat the Christmas stories as parables:
They're meaningful tales, but they never really happened.[4] However,
there are several problems with these conclusions.

First, one of the reasons the scholars have decided that the
infancy stories are fictional is the perceived contradictions between

Luke's and Matthew's versions.[5] Inconsistencies in different versions of a story, however, are not necessarily evidence that the stories are all fabricated. It could be that the different storytellers simply got some of the details wrong in what was essentially a factual account.

Indeed, it is far more likely that there would be *no* contradictions or difficulties if the stories were invented. Fiction writers make their facts line up. Two or three people relating the same events are more likely to provide details that clash because they have perceived the event from different perspectives and have remembered it differently.

Some scholars also claim that the stories of Jesus' birth can't be rooted in history because they too obviously fulfill Old Testament prophecies.[6] It is true that Matthew, of the four gospel writers, likes to draw attention to the prophecies he thinks are being fulfilled. The skeptics have two problems with this. First, they don't believe it is possible for someone to prophesy the future. Secondly, they suspect that the author of Mathew's gospel invented stories deliberately to fulfill the prophecies.

I will deal with prophecies in more detail in chapter seven, but an author's invention or re-arrangement of some details to make his story fulfill certain prophecies does not prove that the story is a complete invention. Furthermore, when one considers the prophecies that the supposedly fabricated Magi story is said to fulfill, it is surprising that Matthew did not do a better job.

For example, one of the Old Testament prophecies that is supposed to be fulfilled by the Magi story is from the sixtieth chapter of the prophet Isaiah: "[T]he wealth of nations shall come to you. Caravans of camels shall cover you, dromedaries of Midian and Ephah; All from Sheba shall come bearing gold and frankincense and heralding the praises of the Lord."[7] If the writer of Matthew's gospel was inventing the story to prove Jesus' birth was a miraculous fulfillment of prophecy, why didn't he add the details about camels and omit the gift of myrrh so his story would match the prophecy more precisely?

Supernatural Nonsense?

Finally, the skeptical scholars reject the possibility that the infancy stories about Jesus could be historical because they contain supernatural elements.[8] The first problem with this is that the skeptics simply assume supernatural experiences are impossible. Any story that contains supernatural elements must therefore be a fanciful invention.

They seem to miss the point that the stories in the Bible are about religious experiences, and religious experiences, by their very definition, have to do with the supernatural. It is true that some of the supernatural elements are more astounding and difficult to believe than others, but religious literature is *about* the supernatural.

Sacred texts are concerned with religion, and religion is about the encounter between divinity and humanity. Removing the supernatural from religious literature is like removing the ball from the game of baseball. When you do, there is no longer a game.

Whether scientifically biased skeptics believe in them or not, supernatural religious experiences are a part of universal human experience. People of every language, religion, and ethnic group down through history have reported experiences they regard as supernatural. A good scholar therefore includes reports of such experiences in his data. He doesn't have to be gullible and swallow them whole, but he should take them seriously and analyze them with respect.

The second problem with the skeptics' approach to the Nativity narratives is that a person's attribution of an unusual experience to a supernatural cause does not mean that he did not have the unusual experience. These unusual experiences are the stuff of religion, and for a scholar of religion to dismiss them simply because they seem difficult to accept is shortsighted and narrow-minded. Furthermore, dismissing a whole story as an invention simply because it has problematic supernatural elements does not inspire confidence in a scholar's ability to see clearly and weigh the facts objectively.

Whether it is a near-death experience, a paranormal experience, or something less dramatic, people retell the amazing things which have happened to them in ordinary life. For example, Aunt Sally tells how she was healed at the summer camp revival meeting by Jesus Christ himself, or Cousin Jimmy tells how he was miraculously preserved from falling headlong into a pot of acid by his guardian angel.

One does not have to accept the miraculous element of the story to acknowledge that Cousin Jimmy really did almost fall into a pot of acid, and that two workmates saw it happen at Florsheim Fertilizer Plant in Hudson Falls, Missouri, on January 27 at three o'clock in the afternoon.

One does not have to accept that Aunt Sally was miraculously healed by Jesus to accept that she really did go to the Hosanna Camp Meeting led by Pastor Bob Johnson on August 3 and that she went in feeling sick and came out feeling better. In other words, it is perfectly possible that a human story that is reported as having miraculous elements might be historical even if the supernatural dimension of the story is questionable.

The third problem with the skeptical scholars' dismissal of the stories because of their supernatural element is that, once they have dismissed them, they will not consider them again. This is what has happened to the story of the Magi.

In the early twentieth century, Biblical scholars began to write off the stories of Jesus' birth—especially the story of the wise men—as pious fantasies. They did so without considering whether the stories might at least be rooted in real events, so they never did the necessary research to uncover the historical element buried beneath layers of legend. Once they decided, based on their preconceived notions, that the stories were not historical, they didn't give the question a serious consideration.

Exploration of the historical basis of the Magi story therefore became an academic no-go zone. When one's academic reputation might be at stake, one's motivation to challenge the received academic wisdom is weak. If a majority of one's respected peers and professional superiors take a particular position, it is easier and better for one's career not to dissent.

Happily, I don't have an academic career to consider. I'm an amateur scholar and freelance sleuth. I'm delighted that our quest to discover the identity of the wise men will require some courage and the ability to think outside the box. We're going to challenge the academic orthodoxy with a kind of cheerful chutzpah.

To do this, we are going to suspend our disbelief in the supernatural elements of the story. This does not mean we accept the supernatural elements at face value. We simply put them to one side and keep an open mind.

Maybe something unusual happened with a star. Maybe not. Maybe someone received supernatural guidance in a dream. Maybe not. We're going to allow that something supernatural may have happened, but we're also going to be skeptical and look for every natural explanation first.

How to Read the Bible

To begin our detective work we must go to the most ancient source of the story: the second chapter of the gospel according to Matthew. Before we start, however, it is important to understand *how* to read the Bible. The Bible is not an ordinary book. It is not like a modern novel or biography or work of history. Instead it is a collection of ancient texts. The New Testament dates from the time of the Roman Empire, and the first part of the Bible—the Old Testament— takes us back many centuries into the history of the Jewish people.

The Bible therefore comes to us from a radically different world. To understand the New Testament, we have to read it as much as possible as the first-century Christians read it. When we go to see a play by Shakespeare, we can best appreciate it if we not only acquaint ourselves with the Elizabethan diction but also study the plot, the characters, and the historical period of the author. The more we know about Shakespeare and his time, the richer our experience of his play will be.

It's the same with reading the Bible. If we read the New Testament assuming that it is like a twenty-first-century history book, we'll be disappointed. If we assume that the Christians of first-century Palestine shared our worldview, we'll get it wrong. If we assume that the text is as accurate, objective, and well researched as a modern documentary film or biography, we will have missed the point.

Instead, we try as much as possible to read the Bible with the mindset of first-century Christians. They assumed that the stories they were being told not only expressed the truth about their religion but were also true historically. They trusted the authors. They understood that details might be missing, characters confused, and chronologies altered, but they also worked on the assumption that the storytellers were essentially trustworthy.

From that basis we can bring our twenty-first-century sensibilities to bear on the texts. We live in a scientific age. When we're told that angels appeared in the night sky and sang to shepherds or a star guided travelers on their journey across the desert, some of us scratch our heads with disbelief. There's nothing wrong with that as long as we approach the gospels on their own terms.

Everyone can admit that they were not written as strictly historical documents, but neither are they fables or fairy tales. Ancient peoples did not see the same division between the "natural" and "supernatural" that we do. For them the visible and the invisible worlds were intermingled. The gospels, following on the Old Testament and consistent with their Jewish origins, include much that is verifiable history, but they also have otherworldly elements.

Furthermore, the evangelists were not concerned with maintaining critical distance or journalistic objectivity. They intended to record what actually happened because those events demonstrated, they believed, that Jesus was the Son of God. As Erasmo Leiva-Merikakis explains, "we must conclude, then, that the genre of the Gospel is not that of pure 'history'; but neither is it that of myth, fairy tale, or legend. In fact, *evangelion* [gospel] constitutes a genre all its own, a surprising novelty in the literature of the ancient world."[9]

Historians therefore allow for what they call "mythological" elements woven into these essentially historical documents. Whether the miracles or the mythological elements happened as the gospels report is open to debate. Believers accept the possibility of the miraculous. Non-believers do not. In each case their assumptions will affect their conclusion.

Moving to Matthew

With all this in mind, we are in a position to investigate the mystery of the Magi. To do that we need to start with the primary evidence—the story as it is related in Matthew's gospel. We'll allow that there may be legendary or myth-like elements to the tale, but we'll take the story at face value.

We won't assume that the whole story is historically true in every detail, but neither will we assume that the whole story is fanciful. Instead, we'll maintain an open mind and attempt an objective consideration of the evidence. The first step in the quest to discover the true identity of the Magi, therefore, is to discover the truth about Matthew and his gospel.

CHAPTER TWO

Matthew: Man of History

To pin down the true identity of the Magi we must first understand the primary source of the story: the gospel according to Matthew. To grasp why the story of the Magi was important to Matthew and his audience, we have to understand the mind of Matthew and his world, and we can't understand that unless we know when Matthew lived and wrote his gospel.

Most people who take the Bible at face value assume that the gospel bearing Matthew's name was written by Jesus' disciple of that name a few years after Jesus' death in AD 33. If they remember their Bible stories, they'll identify him as the tax collector who was also called Levi. New Testament scholars, however, have shown that it is not quite that easy.

Books can be based on various sources and go through different versions, some by the original author and others by later editors. To understand the gospel of Matthew, we have to pick through the process of editing and the question of authorship. Did Jesus' disciple Matthew really write the book a short time after Jesus' death?

The earliest direct written record we have about the author of Matthew's gospel comes from a bishop in Gaul (modern France) named Irenaeus around the year AD 180. Just one generation removed from the apostles themselves, Irenaeus was taught by Polycarp, who was taught by Jesus' disciple John.

Irenaeus wrote, "Matthew also published a gospel, written among the Hebrews in their own language, while Peter and Paul were preaching the gospel and founding the church in Rome."[1] The historian Eusebius, bishop of Caesarea in Palestine, writing in the early fourth century, records an even earlier witness—Papias, a bishop of Hierapolis in Asia Minor, who lived just fifty or sixty years after the death of Jesus. Drawing on those who knew the apostles, Papias asserted that "Matthew set in order the *logia* [sayings] of Jesus in a Hebrew dialect."[2]

The New Testament scholar David Turner believes that "set in order the sayings" means that Matthew collected and organized the oral traditions about Jesus that were circulating in the area of Jerusalem and Judea (what is now southern Israel), and that the "dialect" could refer to Aramaic—the everyday language of Jesus and his disciples.[3]

Furthermore, when Papias refers to the "sayings" of Jesus, he probably means "the things said and done."[4] This earliest evidence about the origin of Matthew's gospel is supported by every other writer of the ancient period of the Christian church, including Ignatius of Antioch (d. AD 107), Tertullian (d. AD 220), and Origen (d. AD 254). In fact, none of the writers of the earliest age disagrees with Papias that Matthew set down the sayings of Jesus in Hebrew or Aramaic.[5]

Jerome, in the late fourth century, claimed to have a copy of Matthew's Hebrew gospel in his monastery in Bethlehem. And the New Testament scholar Wilhelm Schneemelcher shows that Clement of Alexandria (d. AD 215), Origen, and Eusebius had all seen copies of the early version of Matthew's gospel in Hebrew.[6] It's not quite as easy as all that, however.

Irenaeus and Papias say Matthew wrote his collection of sayings in Hebrew or Aramaic, but the Gospel of Matthew that we now have was written in Greek. (For simplicity's sake, I will use "Hebrew" as shorthand for "Hebrew or Aramaic" when referring to Matthew's original collection of sayings.) Most scholars have therefore concluded that the gospel was composed by someone other than Matthew decades later than first thought. In 2009, however, the New Testament scholar James Edwards overturned established theories by showing that Matthew, or perhaps a later writer, wrote an updated version in Greek of the Hebrew collection of sayings and stories.[7]

The detective work becomes more intriguing because much of the language in Matthew's gospel is virtually identical to that in Mark's gospel, leading scholars to suppose that the author of the Greek version of Matthew's gospel used Mark's account as a source, adding Mark's stories to Matthew's original Hebrew collection of sayings for a more complete gospel story.

Because the story of the Magi is found only in Matthew's gospel, some scholars conclude that it must have been added by a later editor to embellish the tales of Jesus' birth. Of course, the story might just as well have been part of Matthew's earlier Hebrew collection of stories and sayings, which the author of Mark's gospel did not have.

If the stories and sayings found only in Matthew's gospel date back to that older, Hebrew redaction of oral traditions, then they are among the earliest recorded and must have come from people who had first-hand knowledge. As the renowned New Testament scholar Raymond Brown—no traditionalist—concluded, "The simplest explanation of the pre-Mathean background of the magi story is that it is factual history passed down from the time of Jesus' birth in family circles."[8]

Detecting the Dates

Unfortunately, the writers of the New Testament did not put a date at the top of their papers. Nevertheless, because they mention certain externally verifiable events, with a bit of sleuthing, we can date the writing of the gospels fairly accurately.

To do so, we begin with the latest possible date for a document and work our way back to the earliest possible date. First, we know that the second (Greek) edition of Matthew's gospel must have been completed before the end of the first century—fewer than seventy years after the death of Jesus. We know this because Matthew's gospel is quoted in the writings of Ignatius, the bishop of Antioch who died in the year 107.

The older (Hebrew-Aramaic) version of Matthew's gospel must have been compiled forty or fifty years earlier, a conclusion we reach by considering some other important events within the first few decades after Jesus died. The most pivotal is the destruction of Jerusalem by the Romans in AD 70. In the twenty-fourth chapter of his gospel, Matthew records Jesus' prophecy of the destruction of Jerusalem, but he never mentions its fulfillment—a silence that is highly significant. The destruction of their sacred capital by the hated Romans was a gigantic calamity in the history of the Jews. The Roman soldiers crucified thousands of Jewish rebels after a terrible siege, and the Roman army finally leveled the city, including the Jews' beloved temple. The destruction of Jerusalem was more cataclysmic for them than the attacks of September 11, 2001, were for the United States.

Why would Matthew not have mentioned such a momentous event when Jesus had predicted it? Almost certainly because it had not yet happened. Matthew is nothing if not enthusiastic about the fulfillment of prophecy. He often points out an incident that he thinks fulfills a prophecy, and he is also intent on showing Jesus to be in the line of the Jewish prophets. If Matthew wanted to show Jesus to be a miracle-working prophet, he would most certainly have mentioned that Jesus' prophecy about the destruction of the temple had come true in the terrible events of AD 70.

Because Matthew does not mention the destruction of Jerusalem, we can deduce that his gospel must have been completed before AD 70. If we dig a bit deeper, however, we'll find that Matthew's first collection of sayings and stories about Jesus goes back even further.

Details and Data

Everyone loves a good detective story. Gathering clues, sifting data, and making connections are vital for dating ancient documents. The dating of Matthew's gospel will depend on another date, and at this point the puzzle gets a bit complicated but intriguing.

As I have pointed out, most scholars believe that the writer of Matthew's gospel used Mark's gospel as a source. If he did, then to date the expanded Greek version of Matthew's gospel accurately, we need to know when Mark's gospel was written. Having thus determined a date for the Greek version of the gospel of Matthew, we can then work back from there to estimate when his collection of Jesus' sayings in Hebrew was compiled.

Papias records that Mark wrote his gospel based on the stories he had heard from the apostle Peter. We know from the New Testament that Mark was Peter's traveling companion,[9] and that Mark was a companion of Paul as well.[10] We also know that Peter and Paul died in Nero's persecution of Christians in Rome around AD 65.[11] Peter, the leading apostle, was a dominant figure in the early Church, yet Mark, who was with him in Rome, does not record his death. We can conclude, then, that Mark's gospel must have been written before Peter's death.

Even more interesting is the dating of the gospel of Luke. Some scholars believe that like Matthew, Luke used Mark's gospel as a source. Like Mark, Luke was a traveling companion of Paul. He wrote not only the gospel bearing his name but also a sequel, the Acts of the Apostles, which records the missionary efforts of Peter and Paul.

The Acts of the Apostles does not mention the destruction of Jerusalem in AD 70, the deaths of Peter and Paul around AD 65, or the beginning of Nero's persecution in AD 64. Now, the heroism of the martyrs, who followed Christ's example even to death, was enormously important for the early Christians. Peter's martyrdom *is* mentioned in John's gospel,[12] and in Acts, Luke records the martyrdoms of Stephen and James. But Acts ends with Paul under house arrest in Rome. Because there is no mention of Paul's death or the beginning of the persecution by Nero, it seems reasonable to conclude that Acts must have been completed before AD 64.

Luke's gospel was written before the Acts of the Apostles.[13] Therefore, splicing together the evidence, we know that if Luke used Mark's gospel as a source, and if he completed both Acts and his gospel before the year AD 64, then Mark's gospel also had to have been written before AD 64. Furthermore, if the scholars are correct that Matthew used Mark for the Greek version of his gospel, then the Greek version of Matthew's gospel was also composed prior to AD 64.[14] Matthew's Hebrew collection of sayings and stories must therefore have been compiled even earlier—probably between the years AD 50 and AD 55, and some scholars place it as early as the decade before.[15]

With such an early date—just ten or twenty years after the death of Jesus Christ in AD 33, there is no reason why the core of Matthew's gospel could not have been written by Matthew the disciple of Jesus, just as the earliest writers—Papias, Irenaeus, and others—attest.[16]

Why does this matter in our search for the Magi? Because the later the date of Matthew's gospel, the more likely the story of the Magi is to be a pious legend devised by someone other than Matthew. An anonymous editor or writer distant from Jesus and the people who knew him might be more inclined to create stories to support a theological point.

If, however, it was Matthew the apostle who began to collect the stories and sayings of Jesus that were circulating just ten or twenty years after his death, then it is probable that the story of the Magi originated with people close to the actual events. If this is so, it is far less likely that the story of the Magi is a mere fable.

Are the gospels based on eyewitness accounts? As one respected Biblical scholar puts it, "quite a few scholars believe that the gospels, if not written by one of Jesus' disciples, nevertheless reflect genuine reminiscences by these disciples that were preserved in their Christian communities."[17] Meanwhile, in *Jesus and the Eyewitnesses: The Gospels as Eyewitness Testimony*, Richard Bauckham of the University of St. Andrews presents a detailed case for the gospels' foundation in first-hand accounts. The Jewish New Testament scholar David Flusser agrees: "My research has led me to the conclusion that the Synoptic gospels [Matthew, Mark, and Luke] are based on one or more non extant early documents composed by Jesus' disciples and the early church in Jerusalem."[18]

If the Magi story is just pious fiction, then our detective work has ended. But if the story might be rooted in eyewitness accounts of historical events, we must press on in our quest to discover the identity of the wise men. If we uncover plausible candidates and all the facts fit, then the skeptics are wrong, and their understanding of the Magi story and the rest of the infancy narratives will need to be revised.

The Mind of Matthew

Having done the detective work, we have little reason to doubt that the core elements of the Gospel of Matthew were compiled by Jesus' disciple Matthew.[19] The evidence is strong that Matthew's stories about Jesus were collected only ten or twenty years after Jesus' death. They were most likely collated from notes taken by his disciples and the word-of-mouth traditions that had been circulating in Judea since his death.[20]

It is probable, then, that the story of the wise men is rooted in a shared memory of the earliest Jewish Christians in Judea, and that probability increases when we consider the context of Matthew's writing. Most scholars agree that Matthew's gospel was addressed to Jewish Christians in Judea or Syria. An audience that close to the events of the gospel would have sniffed out any fabricated stories. To put it bluntly, if the story of the Magi was a fairy tale, the Jewish Christians living where the events had taken place just ten or twenty years earlier would have called the writer's bluff.

We're almost ready to start looking for the wise men, but first we have to discern the mind of Matthew. Understanding not only *what* Matthew wrote but also *why* he wrote is essential to solving the mystery of the Magi.

Matthew the Jew

Most importantly, Matthew was a Jew writing for Jews. We know that he was writing for fellow Jews because, unlike Mark, who was writing for Gentile Christians, he doesn't bother to explain Jewish customs and laws. He quotes the Old Testament more than the other gospel writers and carefully links the events of Jesus' life to the Old Testament prophecies of a coming savior called the Messiah.

At the time Matthew was writing, the nascent Christian Church was struggling with a huge controversy. Its leader, Peter, had had a vision that convinced him that the message of Jesus Christ was supposed to be taken not only to the Jews but to the Gentiles as well.[21] Peter and his brother apostles commissioned Paul to be the "Apostle to the Gentiles." Why was this a problem?

It was a problem because the Jews, who for centuries had thought of themselves as God's chosen people, considered the Gentiles to be dogs. To the men of the ancient world, a dog was not a cute puppy. A dog was a filthy, flea-bitten scavenger. How could Jesus' message and mission also be for the Gentile dogs? Such a thought was revolutionary, disgusting, and unthinkable. These unclean peoples, moreover, had invaded the Jews' Promised Land and oppressed them. Suddenly, everything was changed, and the filthy dogs were also God's chosen ones.

Matthew had the task of convincing his fellow Jews not only that Jesus was the long-looked-for Messiah but also that the Gentiles were part of God's plan.

The second thing to remember is that Matthew's audience of Jewish Christians in the first years after Jesus' death and resurrection—a small underground group—were persecuted by the Romans for being Jews and by their fellow Jews for being Christians. We will see later why appreciating this double persecution is crucial to understanding Matthew's telling of the Magi story.

Tools for Detecting the Truth

If the first version of Matthew's gospel was written ten or twenty years after the death of Jesus by the disciple of that name, then we need to ask whether it might have included the story of the Magi. Most Biblical scholars contend that the stories about Jesus' birth are too full of contradictions and mythical elements to have any foundation in historical events.[22] But have the scholars and skeptics done all their homework?

In the vast realm of Biblical scholarship, one finds surprisingly little research and writing on the stories of Jesus' birth, and almost none of it takes seriously the possibility that the story of the wise men is historical. The work that has been done is biased, out of date, and based on false assumptions and wrong conclusions. Even the scholars' own tools for determining the authenticity of a story have not been used.

To determine whether a particular story in the New Testament might be historical, scholars use certain tools of deduction. The first of these is the "criterion of dissimilarity": If a gospel depicts Jesus saying or doing something that clashes with the Jewish religion of his day, and therefore with the religion of the first Jewish Christians—that is, something that would have made believers uncomfortable—then it is more likely to be authentic.

For example, since it was unheard of for a rabbi to engage a woman in conversation alone, the story of Jesus with the woman at the well in Samaria is unlikely to have been made up. Another example is the parable of the Good Samaritan, in which a person the Jews despised turns out to be the hero. The stories of Jesus' accepting the hospitality of sinners or breaking the Sabbath laws with his disciples likewise meet the "criterion of dissimilarity."

According to the criterion of dissimilarity, the Magi story should be authentic. Why? Because its depiction of non-Jews coming to worship the Jewish Messiah clashes with what good Jews and good Christians from a Jewish background would have expected. They were convinced that the Messiah was for the Jews, not the Gentiles. The story of pagan Magi coming to worship the Christ Child is so improbable that Matthew is unlikely to have made it up.

The scholars' second tool is "the criterion of embarrassment": If a saying or event would have been embarrassing to the memory of Jesus, the apostles, or the early Christians, it is more likely to be authentic. Jesus' losing his temper and clearing out the temple and his allowing a prostitute to pour perfume on his feet and wash them with her tears are examples of stories that meet this criterion, as are stories in which the apostles appear proud, vain, stupid, or unbelieving. The story of Jesus' baptism is likely to be authentic because its depiction of his apparent subordination to John the Baptist would be embarrassing for those who wished to portray Jesus as the preeminent Son of God. The same can be said about his apparently illegitimate birth and his execution as a criminal. Would the story of the Magi have embarrassed the early church?

It would. The Jews considered all foreign religions to be false religions and believed they involved the worship of demons. Foreign magicians were thought to engage in necromancy and witchcraft, sins that carried the penalty of death in the Jewish law. Such people were not supposed to worship the Messiah. That foreign astrologers came to honor the infant Jesus would have been an embarrassment, and therefore it is not likely that the story of the Magi is a pious fantasy invented by the gospel writer.[23]

The third criterion that scholars apply is that of "cultural and historical congruency": A story is less credible if it contradicts known historical facts or if it conflicts with cultural practices common in the period in question. If, on the other hand, the account matches the known historical facts, it is more likely to be authentic. Therefore, when a gospel story fits neatly into what we know of the politics, geography, history, and culture of the time, the story is more likely to be authentic.

Here is where many modern Biblical scholars have been most remiss. Assuming that the Magi story is pious fiction, they have not bothered to investigate the political, historical, geographical, and cultural details that support the historical accuracy of the story of the Magi. Unlocking those details will reveal much about Matthew's world and show how the visit of the Magi to Bethlehem fits perfectly with what we know about the historical circumstances of the birth of Jesus of Nazareth.

Filtering Fact and Fiction

The figure of Santa Claus that we have today is a fanciful development from historical facts about Saint Nicholas of Myra. The story of the wise men developed in a similar way. Elaborations of the Magi story influenced the early Christians, and by the Middle Ages several full-blown mythical versions of the stories had become part of the accepted Christmas tradition.

In the Middle Ages most Christians did not have access to a Bible. They believed the elaborate stories about the sages named Melchior, Balthasar, and Caspar who followed a magical star from exotic distant lands. They heard the various non-Biblical stories about the Magi and lost track of the simple Bible story. Unfortunately many of these accretions are still part of the Magi story today, and they make the story of the wise men sound almost as fanciful as Santa Claus.

In this chapter we sorted through the evidence to determine that Matthew's simple account was part of an early collection of sayings and stories about Jesus. It is perfectly reasonable to conclude that Matthew's version of the Magi story is not only ancient but part of the earliest oral traditions in the Christian church from the region of Judea, where Jesus lived, worked, and taught.

How did the simple story in Matthew's gospel become so elaborate? Why did the Christians over the next five hundred years embellish the story? The answers to these questions will help us cut through the fanciful tales to discover the true identity of the wise men.

CHAPTER THREE

Fantastic Flights of Fantasy

In J. R. R. Tolkien's *The Fellowship of the Ring*, Galadriel explains how knowledge of the ring was lost: "History became legend. Legend became myth." The same could be said of Matthew's wise men.

The story of the kings Balthasar, Caspar, and Melchior laying aside everything to embark on a long and perilous journey, guided across the desert by a magical star, has all the ingredients of an epic adventure—exotic strangers, fabulous riches, danger, faith, and hope. The three kings joining the humble shepherds to worship the Christ child symbolize the equality of Christians in the eyes of the God who became poor for our sake. The kings worship the King of Kings and the shepherds adore the Good Shepherd.

But did it really happen?

The account in Matthew's gospel is straightforward and simple. But the tale of the wise men who followed the star was a rich seam to be mined. There was too much symbolism, mystery, and mysticism to be dismissed. Soon the story of the foreign visitors to Bethlehem was being augmented, and like all good stories, it spread, and as it spread, the simple story became embellished, exaggerated, and exploited.

By the Middle Ages the elaborate versions of the Magi story were accepted as historical. When, in the fifteenth century, the Scriptures began to be translated and printed in the language of the people, it was natural to read into Matthew's simple story the amplifications that had, for centuries, been accepted as fact. Even today, many accept those ancient traditions as "gospel truth."

The problem is, Matthew's version of events does not feature many of the elements of the Magi story we take for granted. To find the kernel of historical truth we must strip away the legendary and mythical accretions. To do that we have to understand what those accretions are and how and why they developed.

Bible Books and Bogus Authors

The official New Testament consists of twenty-seven books: four gospels, a history of the missionary efforts of Christ's Apostles, twenty-one letters, and a visionary book of poetry and prophecy. It is easy to take the Bible for granted, forgetting that in the early years of the church there were many other Christian writings in circulation.

The burgeoning Christian congregations across the Roman Empire circulated other letters, liturgies, gospels, and books of instruction and history. The process by which the Christians eventually decided which books would be included in the New Testament took some time and involved heated debate. There is evidence from around the year 200 that most of the twenty-seven books had been decided on, and certainly by the mid-300s most Christians agreed on which writings should be in the New Testament and which should be excluded.[1]

The exclusion of certain early writings from the New Testament doesn't mean they were worthless or heretical. They were simply found not to be among the oldest Christian writings or to have originated with the apostles of Jesus. Some of these extracanonical writings, like the *Shepherd of Hermas* or the letters of Clement of Rome and Ignatius of Antioch, date from the first generation after the apostles and were often read in church as the Scriptures are today.

Other early writings, however, are suspect. Some of them might have tenuous links with an apostle, but most of them date from a later time and are pseudonymous—that is, they were falsely attributed to an apostle to give them an air of authority. These writings are called "apocryphal," which means "hidden away," because, as the canon of authentically inspired writings was officially defined, the bogus writings were dismissed. These apocryphal epistles and gospels were rejected not only because of their later composition and dubious authorship but also because they attributed to Jesus and his Apostles things they never taught or did—many of them bizarre and fantastic.

The apocryphal accounts of Jesus' birth were particularly popular, and as time passed they became increasingly fanciful. In other words, as Christianity spread across the Roman Empire, Matthew's simple account of the Magi became legend, and the legend became myth.

From History to Legend

The earliest apocryphal account of Jesus' birth is the so-called Gospel of James (not to be confused with the canonical epistle of James), also called the Protoevangelium.[2] Most scholars date it from the middle of the second century. Some suggest that it is rooted in the experience of the first Christians around Jerusalem and that it may well have a foundation in the teachings of Jesus' kinsman, the apostle James, who was the leader of the church in Jerusalem.

The Protoevangelium tells the story of Mary's birth and childhood, her betrothal to Joseph, and the birth of Jesus. Its account of Jesus' birth follows Matthew's and Luke's, but there are some extra details: Mary rides a donkey to Bethlehem, there is no mention of an inn as such, and the stable where Jesus is born is in a cave. Mary is attended in childbirth by a midwife named Salome, and as Jesus is born, a mysterious light appears. Obviously quoting Matthew, the author of the Protoevangelium includes the story of the wise men, adding that the star was so bright on its appearing that all the other stars dimmed in its light.

Ignatius of Antioch (d. AD 108), in his epistle to the Ephesians, waxes eloquent about the star: "A star shone in the night brighter than all other stars. Its light was indescribable, and its strangeness produced wonder. And all the rest of the stars with the sun and the moon made a choir around that star which outshone them all."[3] The transformation into legend of Matthew's simple story of visiting Magi had begun.

And there was more, much more, to come.

Matthew does not suggest that the wise men were kings, but by the third century this idea was starting to get traction as theologians like Tertullian and Origen mused on the Old Testament prophecies that kings would come to worship the Messiah bringing gifts of gold and frankincense.[4] In Psalm 72 they read, "The kings of Tarshish and the Isles shall offer gifts, the kings of Arabia and Seba shall bring tribute. All kings shall pay Him homage, all nations shall serve Him," and Isaiah had prophesied, "Caravans of camels shall fill you, dromedaries from Midian and Ephah; all from Sheba shall come bearing gold and frankincense, and proclaiming the praises of the Lord" (Isaiah 60:6).

From Legend to Myth

Still in the third century, the Magi story began its ascent from legend to myth. "The Legend of Aphroditianus"[5] is an apocryphal writing that originated in Syria, where there was a strong Persian influence. It begins with a miracle in the temple of a pagan goddess in Persia at the time of Christ's birth. The statues in the temple dance and sing and announce that the goddess Hera has been made pregnant by Zeus.

Suddenly a star appears above the statue of Hera, a voice from heaven is heard, and all the dancing statues fall on their faces. The wise men of the court take this sign to mean that a king has been born in Judah—an interpretation that the god Dionysus confirms— and the king of Persia sends the Magi to Judea with gifts. The story recounts their journey to Bethlehem following the star, their meeting with the Jewish leaders, and their encounter with Mary and Jesus. They return to Persia with a portrait of Jesus and Mary, which they put in the temple where the star first appeared.

The legend of Aphroditianus is important because it reveals the connection early Christians were making between the Magi in Matthew's gospel and the magi of Persia. Somewhat earlier, Clement of Alexandria (d. AD 215) had linked the Magi to Persia and to ancient prophecies about a coming savior by the Persian prophet Zoroaster.[6] An Arabic infancy gospel from the sixth century[7] continues this theme, depicting the Magi's journey to Bethlehem as the fulfillment of a Zoroastrian prophecy. Mary gives the wise men Christ's swaddling clothes as a blessing, and the star, now a heavenly angel, directs them home. Zoroastrians were said to worship fire. So upon their return the wise men throw the swaddling clothes on the sacred fire. When the fire goes out, the rags are found to be unharmed, so they put them on their head and eyes before placing them among their treasures.

Clearly, the Magi story had found its wings and soared to mythical heights impossible to imagine by the simple storyteller Matthew.

The Magi Myths and Mani

It is understandable that details might have been added to Matthew's simple story over time, but the fevered elaboration of the tale into the most fantastic myths was the result of its being taken up by Gnostic teachers. A bit like today's New Age religion, ancient

Gnosticism was an undefined mishmash of Christianity, pagan rituals, Jewish occult lore, Eastern esoteric religions, superstitious devotions, and arcane philosophies.

The word "Gnostic" comes from the Greek *gnosis*—"knowledge"— and Gnostic believers relied on the mastery of occult knowledge to attain salvation. The Magi story was a natural fit for the Gnostics. A *magus*, after all, is a magician. For those who were entranced by mystery cults, the masters of wisdom, exotic Persian Zoroastrian priests, made perfect mystical gurus. That they had come to pay homage to the infant Christ added to their appeal.

One of the most influential of the Gnostic movements, Manichaeism, started in the very time and place from which the Arabic infancy gospel and the legend of Aphroditianus originated. The prophet Mani, born around AD 216 in Persia to Jewish and Christian parents, blended the emergent Christianity with Zoroastrian theology and traditional Mesopotamian religion. Like Zoroaster's, Mani's complex teachings were dualistic, maintaining that the cosmos was made up of two opposing forces of darkness and light. The Gnostic teachings of Mani were extremely popular in Syria and Persia from the third to seventh centuries.[8]

During this period, the Christian apocryphal writings blended the Magi with Mani. The Syriac *Cave of Treasures*, written between the fourth and sixth centuries, draws on Jewish Kabbalistic writings to lay out a complex, occult history of the world from Adam and Eve. God condemned Adam and Eve to live in a cave where the mystical gifts of gold, frankincense, and myrrh were enshrined. Millennia later, the Magi were led by the star to the cave to retrieve the mystical gifts to present to Adam's descendent, the world's redeemer.[9]

The *Cave of Treasures* appears in another apocryphal text, *The Revelation of the Magi*,[10] written in the voice of the Magi themselves. The wise men are residents of a mythical land called Shir in the Far East. They are the descendants of Seth, the third son of Adam and Eve, who passed on to them a prophecy from his father that one day a star of amazing brightness would appear to announce the birth of

God in human form. Every year the mystical Magi of Shir ascend their holy mountain to the Cave of Treasures, which contains the wisdom of Seth and the treasures of Adam. Here a star brighter than the sun appears to them as a tiny, radiant human, telling them to go on a long journey to Bethlehem. Setting off, they find that the star child accompanies them, removing all obstacles and miraculously providing them with food and protection.

When they arrive at Bethlehem, Mary accuses them of wanting to steal the child, but they inform her that he is the savior of the world. When they return to the land of Shir, they tell their people what has happened, and all rejoice. Many years later, the apostle Thomas appears and baptizes them, and they all live happily ever after.

Myth or Mistake?

While these fairy tales about the wise men are interesting, they expose the very worst tendencies of Gnostic Christianity, which was enchanted by fanciful myths, bogus mysticism, and arcane knowledge.

Gnosticism, which would flourish in various forms during the first five centuries of the Christian era, was already a force during the time of the Apostles. Paul, for example, warned the Colossians not to be taken in by empty philosophies, fanciful stories, and secret knowledge about "the elemental spirits."[11] And he adjured his young disciple Timothy, "Turn away from godless chatter and the opposing ideas of what is falsely called knowledge, which some have professed and in so doing have departed from the faith."[12] The epistles of John castigate false teachers who "deny that Jesus Christ is come in the flesh"[13]—in other words, those who deny that factual history matters when it comes to the story of Jesus of Nazareth.

Paul and John insist that the events of Jesus' life, death, and resurrection are not fanciful fictions but historical fact, in which all sound doctrine must be rooted. To the Corinthians, for example, Paul writes, "If Christ is not raised from the dead your faith is futile,"[14] and "I delivered to you as of first importance what I also received: that Christ died for our sins in accordance with the scriptures, that he was buried, that he was raised on the third day in accordance with the scriptures, and that he appeared to Cephas [Peter], then to the twelve."[15]

Christianity is rooted in the facts of history, not in fanciful fiction, superstition, secret knowledge, and bizarre cosmic theories. While the Protoevangelium rather innocently embellished the original story, tales like *The Revelation of the Magi* and "The Legend of Aphroditianus" are complete fabrications from beginning to end. These Gnostic texts have no value apart from being mildly entertaining historical curiosities. They are as important to the search for Matthew's wise men as Disney's *Sword in the Stone* is to the search for King Arthur.

The Medieval Myth

By the sixth century, Christians may not have fallen for the wildly fantastic stories of the Gnostics, but the idea that the Magi were wise men from Persia had taken root. So in the sixth century we find the Emperor Justinian commissioning the famous mosaic of the three Magi in Ravenna, their pointed Phrygian caps and pantaloons indicating their Persian origins. Similar iconography from the same period is found in Rome at the Church of Santa Sabina and in the catacombs.

The earliest known source for the wise men's names is a late-fifth-century chronicle, composed in Greek in Alexandria and known today only in a (very poor) eighth-century Latin translation, which identifies them as "Bithisarea," "Melichior," and "Gathaspa"—or, as we know them, Balthasar, Melchior, and Caspar, the names with which the figures in Justinian's mosaic are labeled.[16] Two centuries earlier, a Syrian writer had named them Hormizdah, king of Persia; Yazdegerd, king of Saba; and Perozadh, king of Sheba.[17] Syriac Christians had named the Magi Larvandad, Gushnasaph, and Hormisdas.[18] Ethiopians called them Hor, Karsudan,

Fig. 1 Photo showing the mosaic of the Magi commissioned by Emperor Justinian. *Courtesy of Wikimedia Commons.*

Fig. 2 Photo showing Magi door relief in the Church of Santa Sabina. *Courtesy of Wikimedia Commons.*

Fig. 3 Photo showing a fresco of the Adoration of the Magi in the Catacomb of Priscilla. *Courtesy of Wikimedia Commons.*

and Basanater,[19] while the Armenians said they were named, Kagpha, Badadakharida, and Badadilma.[20]

The various ethnic names of the Magi also indicate a broadening of the tradition from the assumption that they were Persian priests. The Syrians, Ethiopians, and Armenians were among the first peoples to accept the Christian message. Their independent Magi traditions attest to the antiquity of their faith and affirm Augustine of Hippo's suggestions that the wise men represented the whole of the Gentile (non-Jewish) world.[21]

Written some two hundred years after Justinian's famous mosaics, an eighth-century Irish manuscript offers more details about the appearance of the wise men, explaining that they represent the three ages of man (youth, middle age, and old age). By this time they were no longer Persian but had assumed racial characteristics indicating that one was European, one African, and one Asian—representing the three regions of the known world.[22] The Venerable Bede, writing in early-eighth-century Britain, mused that the international origins of the three wise men could also signify the three sons of Noah, who, as tradition had it, re-peopled the globe and were the source of humanity's three basic racial groups. He summarized the tale as it was known in his time:

> The Magi were the ones who gave gifts to the Lord. The first is said to have been Melchior, an old man with white hair and a long beard…who offered gold to the Lord as to a king. The second, Gaspard by name, young and beardless and ruddy complexioned,…honored him as God by his gift of incense, an oblation worthy of divinity. The third, black skinned and heavily bearded, named Balthasar,…by his gift of myrrh testified to the Son of Man who was to die.[23]

The legends continued to develop, and according to the twelfth-century life of Saint Eustorgio, the bodies of the three kings were discovered in Persia in the early fourth century by Helena, the mother of the emperor Constantine. The relics were transferred to the great church of Hagia Sophia in Constantinople. When Eustorgio became bishop of Milan, he petitioned the emperor to enshrine the relics of the Magi in his city. In 1164, when Milan was looted by the army of Frederick Barbarossa, the bones of the three kings were removed to Cologne, Germany, where they remain, entombed in the great Gothic cathedral in a magnificent gold and enamel shrine.

In the fourteenth century the Venetian explorer Marco Polo recorded that he had visited the village in Persia where Helena had identified the tomb of the Magi. And in the same century, the Carmelite monk John of Hildesheim, in his *History of the Three Kings*, recounted how the star was first sighted in the forty-second year of the emperor Augustus from the summit of Mount Vaus in the East by a group of pagan astrologers who were aware of the Old Testament prophecy of Balaam.[24]

Fig. 4 Print showing Peter Paul Rubens's *Adoration of the Magi. Courtesy of Wikimedia Commons.*

The star, writes John, was as bright as the sun. Melchior traveled from Nubia and Arabia, Balthasar from Godolia and Saba, and Caspar from Tharsis and Egrisoulle. Each king, with a magnificent retinue, followed the star for thirteen days. Arriving in Jerusalem on the same day, they were amazed to discover that they could understand one another's languages. After their audience with King Herod, and instructed by his scribes, they continued their journey to Bethlehem, again guided by the magical star.

Like the story of Saint Nicholas, who became the modern Santa Claus, the story of the wise men grew into legend and expanded into myth. From Syria and North Africa to Europe and then around the world, Matthew's simple story not only grew but also influenced world culture.

The Modern Myth

The medieval version of the story—with an old man, a middle-aged man, and a youth, each of a different race—influenced virtually all Western Christian art from the late Middle Ages onward. The story of the kings has also influenced cultural understandings and movements within Christian Europe and around the world even to the present day.[25]

In the school Christmas pageant each December you will probably see the three kings portrayed by boys from three different races, just as the kings were portrayed in medieval mystery plays. One may wear a long beard, while another is middle-aged and the third youthful. They will follow a magical star and bear the names of Melchior, Caspar, and Balthasar. It will all be sweet and enchanting, but it owes more to the legends that developed about the Magi than the simple story that Matthew records.

With the rise of Islam in the early seventh century, both Zoroastrianism and Christianity came under a cloud in the Middle East. It is no coincidence that this was the time that Christians stopped portraying the wise men as Persian Zoroastrian priests. By the eighth century, as we have seen, even in remote Ireland and Britain, the Magi had become kings from Europe, Asia, and Africa. As the wise men were universalized, they were untethered from their geographical and historical moorings. It was as if the Magi resided in the realm of mythical meaning, and if anyone asked who they *really* were and where they *really* came from, a learned professor would peer over his glasses and say, "It is likely that, if they truly existed, they were members of the ancient Persian caste of sorcerers and stargazers called magi."

Now in the twenty-first century, that is still the default setting. Most scholars do not think the question of the historical identity of the Magi is even worth asking about, and those who do enquire are usually content with the pat answer that they may have been Persian Zoroastrian priests.

But if they existed, did the Magi come from Persia?

The more one examines that answer, the more the riddle deepens.

CHAPTER FOUR

Sages and Stargazers

The Emperor Justinian's famous mosaics of the Magi in Ravenna—three men in Persian costume labeled Balthasar, Caspar, and Melchior—show that by the sixth century the Magi's Persian identity was widely accepted. The heartland of Christianity at that time was Syria, Turkey, Greece, and southern Italy. Matthew said the wise men came "from the East," so it was natural to conclude that he meant the ancient empire of Persia.

The Greek word Matthew used for "wise men," moreover, was *magoi*, which was borrowed from the Persian *maguš*. Historically, magi were Persian Zoroastrian priests—an ancient caste of influential sages and stargazers. That seems to make a strong case for the Magi's being Persian Zoroastrian priests. Case closed.

Or maybe not.

The identification of the Magi as Persians has been widely assumed but never thoroughly investigated. Who were the Persian magi? What was their history, and, more importantly, where were they and what was their status at the time of Christ's birth? Did they have the motive and the means to go on a long trek to find a newborn Jewish king?

To answer these questions, we must dig more deeply into the political, geographical, cultural, and religious background of the Persian magi. We must also understand their historical context, which means we first need a quick brush-up on the history of the ancient Middle East.

A Six-Paragraph Tour of the Ancient Middle East

If we were to go to Italy and take a time machine back two thousand years we'd find ourselves at the heart of the mighty Roman Empire. If we went back another two thousand years, the center of power would not be Italy but two great river basins: the Nile in Egypt and Mesopotamia, the land "between rivers"—those rivers being the Tigris and the Euphrates—in what is now eastern Iraq. For centuries the world's culture, wealth, and power ebbed and flowed between these two great centers of civilization.

Abraham, the father of the Hebrew nation, lived in Mesopotamia around the year 2000 BC. The next thousand years saw the slavery of the Jews in Egypt, their deliverance under Moses, and their entrance into the Promised Land. King David lived around the year 1000 BC. At that point Egypt was still a great power, and the warlike Assyrians held sway in what is now Iran and Iraq.

Moving forward another five centuries brings us to the crucial date of 586 BC. This is the year that the Neo-Babylonian Empire under the great King Nebuchadnezzar (d. 562 BC), having swept away the Assyrians in the east, conquered Jerusalem, destroying the magnificent temple that David's son Solomon had built and taking the brightest and best of the Jewish people to Babylon as captives.

The Neo-Babylonian Empire was short lived, however, and about fifty years after Nebuchadnezzar conquered Jerusalem, the Persian king Cyrus the Great (d. 530 BC) defeated the Neo-Babylonians and established the Achaemenid Persian Empire. The Old Testament connects with secular history here, for this is the time when the prophet Daniel was active in the court of Nebuchadnezzar and predicted Cyrus's victory.

Based in the ancient city of Babylon and extending across northern Arabia to Egypt and from eastern Europe to India, the Achaemenid Empire was the greatest power the world had yet seen. It lasted two hundred years, until it was conquered by Alexander the Great in 331 BC. For the next one hundred years the Greeks controlled the territory of former Persia-Babylon until they were expelled around 247 BC by local chieftains who established the Parthian Empire.

Meanwhile in the West, as Greek power was fading, Roman power was rising, and by the time of the birth of Jesus of Nazareth the ancient world was dominated by two great empires: the Parthian Empire, occupying the ancient Persian lands in Mesopotamia, and the Roman Empire, encircling the Mediterranean from Europe to North Africa.

Who, then, were the magi, and where did they fit in the ancient world?

Imagining the Magi

One of the earliest mentions of the magi is by the Greek historian Herodotus (d. 425 BC), who says they came from the region of Media, in what is now northwest Iraq and Kurdistan. One of the six original tribes that made up the nation of the Medes,[1] they made their historical appearance during the Neo-Babylonian and Achaemenid periods.

Little is known about the magi before this time, but it would be safe to assume from what we know about the development of religion and their activities in the Neo-Babylonian and Persian empires that the magi began as tribal shamans, soothsayers, astrologers, and medicine men.[2]

The Roman historians Pliny and Tacitus associated them with sorcery and magic,[3] and Pierre Briant, in his definitive history of Persia, describes their functions as "scribes, haruspices, exorcists, doctors, and singers."[4] Jerome, writing in the fourth century, identified three classes of magi: "Some were practitioners of demonic magic, others were experts in astronomy and the science of nature, while a third group was a caste of ascetical priests."[5]

Religion, for modern people, is a mixture of prayer, worship, faith, and good works. We think of religion as a set of doctrines to be believed and commandments to be obeyed. Ancient pagan religion, however, had little to do with creeds or moral codes. For the ancients, religion was about appeasing the gods and using arcane knowledge, magic, and wisdom to predict the future and guarantee good fortune.

Like most pagan priests, the magi offered animal sacrifices and tried to foretell the future by examining entrails, interpreting dreams, and studying the stars. They combined their astronomical wizardry and soothsaying with the healing arts—driving out demons and healing the sick with their knowledge of herbs, potions, and spells.[6] They were the guardians of the ancient wisdom and lore.[7] They were, if you like, the Dumbledores, Merlins, and Gandalfs of their day.

Zoroaster: The Forgotten Prophet

Most Westerners will scratch their head at the odd-sounding name "Zoroaster." Maybe they've heard something about Zoroastrianism, or they might recognize his other name, "Zarathustra," if they are familiar with the work of the philosopher Nietzsche. Otherwise, many will draw a blank. Yet before the Muslim conquest of the

Middle East in the sixth and seventh centuries AD, most of the people of Mesopotamia followed the ancient religion of Zoroastrianism.

The life of the prophet Zoroaster is shrouded in mystery, but many historians believe that in the sixth century BC, around the time Cyrus the Great was establishing the Achaemenid Empire, he was active in Iran. That is the time when the religion of Zoroaster starts to appear formally, so it seems a likely enough period in which to place him.

Zoroaster categorized the primitive Iranian gods as good or evil and taught that there was one god over them all: Ahura Mazda, whose name means "Illuminating Wisdom" or "Wise Lord." For Zoroastrians, Ahura Mazda was the sustaining force of the universe. Like the Jews, the followers of Zoroaster did not worship idols, and they looked forward to the coming of a savior messiah. They also believed in the afterlife of heaven or hell and human free will.[8]

As Cyrus's Achaemenid Empire grew, Zoroastrianism became the official religion, and the primitive cult of the magi evolved as they adopted the teachings of Zoroaster.[9] By the time of Cyrus's son and successor, Cambyses II, the magi had become the official Zoroastrian priests of the Persian Empire. With the teachings of Zoroaster, the magi added a sophisticated theology and enlightened philosophy to their primitive shamanism.[10]

As the Achaemenid Empire gained strength, the magi also grew in power. No longer mere tribal witchdoctors, they had become masters of wisdom, theologians, interpreters of dreams, skilled astrologers, and mathematicians. And Greek philosophy, mathematics, and astronomy have their roots in the wisdom of the Persian magi.[11]

The magi's control of the ancient tribal oral traditions and their scientific and occult knowledge made them influential courtiers, counselors to the king, and educators of the royal progeny. As the empire flourished, so did the fortunes of the Zoroastrian magi. By the time of Cyrus the Great, the king never went anywhere without magian advisors in his entourage.[12] Assuming more and more power, the

Fig. 5 Photo showing a rock carving at Behistun. *Courtesy of the Library of Congress.*

magi eventually were acknowledged as king-makers.[13] No one could hope to gain or retain the throne without the approval of the magi.

The Decline of the Megistane

The magi were at the peak of their influence under Cyrus the Great. In the previous reigns of Nebuchadnezzar and Nabonidus, the magi were a recognized power group within the ruling body known as the Council of the Megistanes, which selected the monarch[14] and, in theory, could check his power and even depose him. Once elected, however, the king had absolute power, and anyone who sought to dethrone him did so at the risk of his life,[15] as the magi would learn after Cyrus's death. Herodotus tells the tale.

Cyrus died in 530 BC and was succeeded by his oldest son, Cambyses II, a capricious and cruel ruler who, fearing for his throne, schemed to have his younger brother Smerdis secretly murdered. In March of 522 BC, however, while Cambyses was away on a military campaign, an imposter—a magus named Gaumata—seized the throne as Smerdis. Confused by this news—he thought Smerdis was dead—and preparing to hurry back to quash the revolt, Cambyses was killed in an accident. The power vacuum allowed the general Darius to sweep into the city and kill Gaumata and his supporters. According to Herodotus, Darius's supporters "then rushed into the streets waving the severed heads of the magi shouting the story to the people. This set off a brief purge with bloodthirsty Persians slaughtering any magi they found."[16] The event was later commemorated with "an annual festival called Magophonia (killing of the Magi) during which Magi were obliged to remain in seclusion or risk death."[17]

The attempted coup by the magi and their subsequent slaughter by Darius marked the first decline of the magi's power. The incident is literally carved in stone at the famous rock face monument of Behistun in Iran. Darius is depicted trampling the head of Gaumata and receiving his enemies in chains, and an inscription in three languages declares, "I with a few men slew that Gaumata the Magian, and those who were his foremost followers." After the slaughter Darius exiled the magi to their native Media, while others fled into Asia Minor, Arabia, and the other territories where later writers record their presence.[18]

This was the first devastating blow to the power of the Persian magi. The continuing power struggles over the next four hundred years reduced their influence even further, until it was a mere shadow of what it had been in their days as courtiers and counselors to the king.

The Rise and Fall of the Magi

Despite their defeat at the hands of Darius, the magi continued to have an advisory presence in his court, and they enjoyed a strong resurgence under the reign of Darius's son Xerxes. They accompanied him in his conquest and destruction of the Greek capital, Athens, in 480 BC.[19]

The tables were turned, however, when Alexander the Great invaded Persia 150 years later and burned the Persian capital of Persepolis. Because the magi hated Alexander and had stirred up rebellion against him, he destroyed their temples and ancient books.[20] As a caste, they were decimated. A Zoroastrian text called the *Greater Bundahishn* records that the Greeks "destroyed all the families of rulers, magi and public men and...extinguished an immense number of sacred fires," virtually destroying the magi, their ancient treasures, and their religion.[21]

Once again the magi were persecuted and dispersed. Little or nothing is heard of them during the Greek domination of their territory in the fourth century BC,[22] but as the Greeks' power waned and the Parthians' power began to grow, the magi enjoyed a slight resurgence.

From Persians to Parthians

The Parthians migrated into Iran in the first half of the third century BC.[23] They were not native Persians rebelling against Greek rule but "unsophisticated immigrants."[24] As the Greeks withdrew, writes the historian Strabo, the land was "full of brigands and nomads" and much of it was deserted.[25] To establish a government the Parthian tribesmen borrowed heavily from Greek ideas and the remnants of the Achaemenid civilization.

When it came to religion, the Parthians "were neither Magians nor Zoroastrians."[26] However, they did adopt a Persian style of government, with a reconstituted Council of the Megistanes.[27] While there were magi involved in the Parthian court, it is unlikely that they were anything more than senior noblemen who were respected for their wisdom and experience. By the mid-first century BC—about thirty years before Jesus' birth—the stability of the Parthian Empire had crumbled and the land was in constant turmoil.

The Parthians, engaged in a running power struggle with Rome, were ruled internally by the ruthless King Phraates IV, who on assuming the throne in 37 BC murdered his father and thirty brothers.[28] Five years into his reign, the Council of the Megistanes, including some of the remaining magi, deposed him, but the coup failed, and the magi's power and influence continued to disintegrate.[29] With the remaining power of the magi waning, the Parthian court descended into insane violence, as one king after another was deposed and murdered.

To be sure, the magi had been powerful courtiers in the early years of the Persian Empire, and they were still known as Zoroastrian priests in the early decades of the Christian era. But because of their involvement in two failed coups and the slaughter by Alexander the Great's forces, by the time of Christ's birth, the magi were a spent force.

The Survival of the Magi

As George Rawlinson, a historian of the Parthian Empire points out, "the Magi fell into disrepute, and if not expelled from their place in the national council, at any rate found themselves despised and deprived of influence."[30] By the time of the birth of Jesus, the Persian magi no longer had the wealth, power, or motivation to set out on a long and costly journey to pay homage to a new king of the Jews.

Furthermore, it is unlikely that Phraates IV would have had any interest in funding such a journey. His throne was insecure, he was preoccupied with his conflicts with Rome, and the magi had been part of the coup to unseat him. Phraates IV had no reason to assist his magian enemies or to take an interest in a newborn king of the Jews.

It is true that at the time of Christ's birth, Phraates IV had just established an uneasy truce with the Romans, agreeing to stay on the eastern side of the Euphrates River.[31] George van Kooten argues that magi from Parthia could have made the journey because of the peace treaty,[32] but that peace was fragile, and Phraates's vindictive and untrustworthy character made the truce an uneasy one. Throughout the previous fifty years, moreover, control of Judea had gone back and forth between the Parthians and the Romans. In 40 BC the Romans re-established control over Judea, replacing a Parthian puppet king with their vassal Herod. Consequently, the Parthians hated Herod, and Phraates IV was unlikely to violate his truce with the Romans to send diplomats to pay homage to an heir of Herod.

So while the Persian magi seem at first glance to be the obvious candidates for Matthew's wise men, an examination of the history makes it clear that they were in fact unlikely to have been the mysterious visitors to Bethlehem. Their influence at a low point, hedged in by Roman military might, they did not have the motive or the means to make such a journey.

The Persian magi were not the only wise men in the ancient Middle East, however. Members of another more mysterious nation during this period were not only known as sages and stargazers, but they also had the means and a very strong motivation to make the journey to Bethlehem.

CHAPTER FIVE

The Riddle of the Nabateans

Elegized as "a rose-red city half as old as time,"[1] Petra tops the bucket list of every tourist to the Middle East. Carved out of red sandstone cliffs in what is now southern Jordan, Petra has a mysterious allure that few other sites can match. The high point of a visit to the desert city is the trek down a narrow cavern to the Khazneh or "Treasury"—the royal tomb made famous as the backdrop for the final scene in *Indiana Jones and the Last Crusade*.

Petra today is a vast archaeological treasure trove that would have delighted Indiana Jones. It is also a world heritage site and Jordan's most popular tourist destination. In her visit to Petra a few years ago, my daughter encountered busloads of tourists from around the world,

Fig. 6 Photo showing The Treasury at Petra. *Courtesy of Wikimedia Commons.*

including a pair of Chinese teenagers dressed as Indiana Jones, complete with leather jackets, felt hats, pistols, and bullwhips.

In addition to the famous treasury, visitors can explore the Roman-style outdoor theater and the ruins of temples and tombs. Standing in the heart of the ancient city, one can visualize a half-mile-long, stone-paved thoroughfare flanked by the important structures of the city's cosmopolitan life. There are remains of luxurious baths and gardens, as well as an open marketplace and, atop the surrounding hills, shrines reached by winding outdoor staircases.

At the time of Jesus' birth, the city of Petra was the thriving capital of the Nabatean kingdom, a major power in the Middle East. Covering most of the Sinai Peninsula and extending halfway along the eastern coast of the Red Sea, the Nabatean kingdom, at its height, spread across northern Arabia and present-day Jordan to Damascus in Syria.

By the first century BC, the fiercely independent Nabateans, dominating the vital trade routes that extended from India across the Arabian Peninsula and the Mediterranean to Egypt, Parthia, and Rome, had become fabulously wealthy.[2] The Nabatean kings fancied themselves equal players on the world stage with the likes of Pompey, Julius Caesar, Herod the Great, and the glamorously decadent Mark Antony and Cleopatra.

In the decades leading up to the birth of Jesus Christ, Petra, like Jerusalem, was a capital city, if not of the first rank, then certainly a first runner-up. Today's visitor to Petra will glimpse the remains of a splendid ancient city, connect with the high drama of the Roman Empire, and catch the spirit of one of the most enterprising and ingenious peoples of the ancient world.

The Ingenious Nabateans

Anyone who wants to dominate the desert must control the water supply, and the Nabateans managed some of the cleverest water systems the world has ever seen. Throughout Petra and the surrounding desert are the remains of the dams and cisterns the Nabatean engineers built to collect and save every drop of water from the natural springs and winter downpours. Aqueducts, canals, and piping systems carried the precious water across mountains, through gorges, and into the temples, homes, and gardens of Petra's citizens.

In the first century BC, the Greek historian Diodorus Siculus admiringly described the hydraulic inventiveness of the Nabateans:

While there are many Arabian tribes who use the desert as pasture, the Nabateans far surpass the others in wealth although they are not much more than ten thousand in number; for not a few of them are accustomed to bring down to the sea frankincense and myrrh and the most valuable kinds of spices, which they procure from those who convey them from what is called Arabia Eudaemon. They are exceptionally fond of freedom; and, whenever a strong force of enemies comes near, they take refuge in the desert, using this as a fortress; for it lacks water and cannot be crossed by others, but to them alone, since they have prepared subterranean reservoirs lined with stucco, it furnishes safety. As the earth in some places is clayey and in others is of soft stone, they make great excavations in it, the mouths of which they make very small, but by constantly increasing the width as they dig deeper, they finally make them of such size that each side has a length of one plethrum. After filling these reservoirs with rain water, they close the openings, making them even with the rest of the ground, and they leave signs that are known to themselves but are unrecognizable by others."³

The Nabateans began to emerge as a civilization in the sixth century BC, and by the late fourth century they had established themselves in the area around Petra (or Reqem, as it was known to them). Although they eventually settled at Petra, they were originally nomadic, moving seasonally across the desert, engaging in trade and moving with their herds in search of water and fresh pasture.⁴

For centuries the nomadic Arabian tribes had traded in frankincense, myrrh, and other native products, but the Nabateans cornered the market. Then through naval and military might, they expanded and consolidated the trading routes across the desert.

Ships sailed across the Indian Ocean to the docks of Yemen laden with "pearls from Bahrain, cotton, ginger and cinnamon from India, and silk from China."[5] Camels were also loaded with ginger, frankincense, myrrh, and gold to cross the Arabian desert to the port of Gaza in Judea, where the goods would be loaded onto ships bound for Rome. On the return journey the Nabatean caravans were bulging with bitumen, henna, storax, asbestos, cloth, silk gauze from Gaza, damask from Damascus, glass, orpiment, gold, and silver.[6] To protect these caravans from bandits, they chose the most challenging routes through the desert, zigzagging through wadis and hidden valleys, up steep cliffs and down narrow chasms. They set up forts at strategic spots, each with secret cisterns to water their camels and provide for their workers.[7]

By the second century BC, the Nabateans had fully developed the city of Petra as the hub of their trading empire. To their trade routes across the desert they added ports along the eastern shore of the Red Sea. Diodorus Siculus tells of sea battles between the Nabateans and Egyptians—the Nabateans no doubt trying to protect their precious cargoes from Egyptian pirates.[8]

The origins of this marvelously ingenious and enterprising people are one of the great mysteries of the ancient Middle East. Scholars have pieced together what evidence they can find, but the Nabateans still seem to have materialized from nowhere in the sixth century BC.

Understanding where and how the Nabateans emerged from history will be crucial in understanding their beliefs, priorities, and motivations. Then as we understand the worldview of the Nabateans, it will become clear why they, and not the Persians, are the most likely nation of origin for Matthew's wise men.

Out of Antiquity

From the earliest times the people of northwest Arabia were nomadic or semi-nomadic shepherds. Among them were the Midianites, Qedarites, Ammonites, Moabites, and Edomites who figure in the Old Testament. Why then, after centuries of this way of life, did one tribe suddenly change its ways in the mid-sixth century BC and begin to settle down, build an opulent city, harness the water supply, establish a monarchy, form a military, and develop a trading empire unrivaled in its wealth?

One of the most mystifying facts about the Nabateans is that, despite their sophistication, they left no written history. As the Arab Biblical scholar Tony Maalouf observes, "Contrary to the norm of many peoples in world history, the community that occupied [Petra] and the regions associated with its kingdom did not leave any record of their history and origin."[9] Why did the Nabateans not leave written records? Some theorize that they had no written language of their own. Yet they did use Aramaic, the international language of their day, so they could have recorded their history as other civilizations did.[10]

In the absence of Nabatean writings, historians must reconstruct their story from archaeological fragments, graffiti, inscriptions, and the second- or third-hand accounts of ancient Greek and Roman writers.[11]

For centuries the Edomite tribe had dominated the area of northwest Arabia where Petra was built, but that situation changed dramatically in the mid-sixth century BC, especially after Nebuchadnezzar's conquest of Jerusalem in 586 BC and the Babylonian captivity of the Jews. Ten years earlier, the Babylonians had invaded northern Arabia,[12] and a few years after the destruction of Jerusalem they conquered the remaining tribes in the area—the Edomite, Moabite, and Ammonite kingdoms.[13] These events allowed the Edomites to move west into Judea, and as they did, the Nabateans occupied the former Edomite territory.[14]

Father Abraham

But who were the Nabateans who suddenly appeared on the scene?

The archaeologist David Graf suggests that they may have originally been a Mesopotamian tribe called the "Nabatu" who fled into northern Arabia in the late eighth century BC as a result of Assyrian attacks.[15] On the other hand, Jean Starcky, a Nabatean scholar, theorizes that they moved north from the southern Arabian tribes.[16] J. R. Bartlett, an expert on the Edomites, is probably right in suggesting that the Nabateans arose out of one of the other ancient tribes of northern Arabia.[17] One of the critical pieces of the puzzle is the ancestry the northern Arabian tribes shared with the Jews.

According to the Old Testament, both the Edomites and the Jews were descended from the patriarch Abraham. The Edomites' ancestor was Abraham's grandson Esau, while the Israelites (the Jews) claimed descent from Esau's twin brother, Jacob. The tribes of Kedar, Ephah, and Midian also claimed descent from Abraham through Ishmael, his son by the slave girl Hagar, and Ishmael's second wife, Keturah (Genesis 25:1).

The Old Testament also mentions a people called the Nebaioth.[18] According to Genesis 28:9, Nebaioth was another grandson of Abraham, through Ishmael. Elsewhere in the Old Testament the Nebaioth are depicted as the most important of the Arabian tribes.[19] So according to the Old Testament traditions, the various northern Arabian tribes, including the Nebaioth, shared their ancestry with the Jews.

Linguists dispute the link between "Nebaioth" and the "Nabateans."[20] But other evidence would seem to support a connection between the Nabateans and the descendants of Abraham's grandson. Certainly, the Nabatean territory in northern Arabia overlaps with the area traditionally occupied by the Edomites and the Nebaioth tribe, and according to Diodorus, the Nabateans and the Nebaioth were both known for their expertise in breeding sheep and goats and for their ingenious water collection and retention technology.[21]

Tony Maalouf summarizes the debate on Nabatean tribal origins: "At present there seems to be enough evidence to identify the Nabateans with North Arabians, who rallied mostly under the Ishmaelite umbrella. The sweeping presence of the Nabateans in North Arabia by the end of the first millennium BC made them representative of the children of Ishmael, whether or not future evidence may equate them with the Nebaioth."[22]

Furthermore, when Moses fled from Egypt after murdering an Egyptian slave driver, he took refuge among the Midianites in northwest Arabia. This was the territory in which the Hebrews lived as nomads before entering the Promised Land, and today's visitor to the area around Petra can visit the purported site of the tomb of Moses' brother Aaron.

Not only did the various tribes of northern Arabia share their ancestry with the Jews, there were also many similarities in their religion and culture. We will see later how these roots in the family and faith of Abraham are crucial to the story of the Magi and to the development of early Christianity.

Migrations and Mergers

Nomadic peoples, by definition, are on the move. Their territories are provisional, their borders porous, and their populations forever in flux. The archaeologist Philip Hammond suggests that in the turmoil of the sixth-century invasions, the Nabateans and the Edomites merged:

> From hints dropped in contemporary literature, from the strange migration of the indigenous Edomites at Petra to the West—where they became known as Idumeans—and from the question of the origin of the rather advanced technologies displayed in Nabatean art, metallurgy, hydraulics, architecture, and other fields, it is possible to recognize in the later Nabatean culture a remarkable blending of two early Arab peoples—the long sedentary Edomites and the vigorous, mercantile, caravaneering Nabateans.[23]

The influence from other tribes was not only from northern Arabia. Jane Taylor observes, "in the centuries that the Nabateans moved through Arabia, they were in contact with many tribes, some nomadic like themselves, others in settled farming communities. A very few, like the [southern Arabian] people of Saba, Mal'in, Qataban, and

Hadhramaut by the sixth and fifth centuries b.c. were spectacularly advanced in architecture and water technology."[24]

These military incursions and subsequent tribal migrations partially explain the origins of the Nabateans, but what brought them together? Why, after living for centuries as nomadic shepherds and traders, did they build a great city? What sparked the development of their impressive agricultural technologies, their architecture, their military prowess, and their achievements in religion, government, and diplomacy?

Refugees from Jerusalem

I believe the rise of the Nabateans can be best explained by the cultural and technological contributions of foreign refugees. As Jane Taylor writes, the Nabateans' "gift was to learn from the skills of others, and to transform disparate ideas into something uniquely their own."[25]

The nomads of northern Arabia were not the only ones to be scattered and resettled in the military upheavals of the sixth century. When Nebuchadnezzar conquered Jerusalem in 586 BC, he did not transport all the Jews to Babylon. Poor farmers remained on the land in Judea, and Josephus records that some of the scattered Jews escaped to Arabia.[26]

The fortress-like settlement of Petra would have provided a congenial refuge. After Nebuchadnezzar's violent victory, writes Iain Browning, "[t]he land on both sides of the Jordan was full of fleeing, broken men seeking refuge from the holocaust. Many made their way to the comparative safety of the high hills of Edom and hid there."[27] The Jewish memory of this migration lived on for centuries, according to Adolf Neubauer: "[T]he medieval Jews of Arabia had a tradition from their ancestors that a great number of them took refuge in North Arabia at the time of the destruction of the first temple by Nebuchadnezzar."[28]

Those fleeing from Nebuchadnezzar's armies would have found fellow Jews already settled in Arabia.[29] "An Israelite colony is supposed to have been formed in Northern Arabia during the reign of David,"[30] and, as Raymond Brown observes, "[c]ommercial relations between Israel and South Arabia went back to Solomon's time…and there were Jewish colonies in Medina [in central Arabia]."[31] Some of the Jerusalem refugees fled to Yemen, where there was already a Jewish enclave.[32] In fact, "[t]he Jewish community of northern Arabia was one of the largest ancient Jewish communities in the history of the Jewish people."[33]

Blood Is Thicker

As we have seen, the tribes of northern Arabia claimed Abraham as a common ancestor with the Jews. One of the discoveries among the Dead Sea Scrolls was the "Genesis Apocryphon," an ancient non-Biblical text that describes Abraham's travels in Mesopotamia and around the coast of Arabia.[34] Abraham's roots in Arabia have also been traced to the oasis town of Tayma, one of the oldest Jewish settlements in Arabia.[35] According to the Old Testament, the town shares the name of another of Abraham's offspring through Ishmael.[36]

The Arabian tribes shared not only their Abrahamic ancestry with the Jews but also their culture. Tony Maalouf traces the history of Jewish wisdom literature to a shared culture with the Ishmaelite tribes of Arabia.[37] Referring to the work of Izhak Ben-Svi, Maalouf writes, "His analysis of names from South Arabia proved that during the Hellenistic and Roman eras there were large communities of Jews and Jewish converts.… Thus it becomes clear that Judaism and Jewish settlements in the Arabia Peninsula were most likely very significant in the post-exilic period."[38]

The British Biblical scholar Margaret Barker has uncovered a Jewish tradition that in the seventh century BC thousands of Jewish priests, fleeing a rigorist purge by King Josiah in Jerusalem, settled in Arabia.[39] The ancient traditions and wisdom of Jews from before the time of Solomon's temple, she maintains, were kept alive in the Arabian settlements by groups of Jewish priestly émigrés. This "first-temple" Judaism was rooted in the Abrahamic faith rather than Mosaic legalism.[40] This earlier form of Judaism was therefore very similar to the religion of the northern Arabian tribes.[41]

But there is more.

God, You Are My Rock

The Old Testament is full of references to God as a solid foundation and sure defense. He is therefore called the "Rock." So the psalmist says, "Blessed be the Lord, my rock."[42] This was not just poetry. The rock was an important symbol for followers of the Abrahamic faith.

In a world where gods and goddesses proliferated and most societies worshipped carved statues of their gods, one of the most striking aspects of Nabatean religion was that it did not feature idols. Instead the Nabatean gods were represented by standing stones. The carved rectangular rocks, four feet by two feet, were smooth and blank.

Later, primitive human features were carved on these stones, and in Greek and Roman times carved idols were introduced. But authentic Nabatean religion did not feature graven images, and there is evidence of stout resistance when Greek and Roman idols were introduced,[43] even "fanatical iconoclasm."[44]

The term for a religion that represents its god as a standing stone is "aniconic." John Healey, an expert in Nabatean religion, identifies the roots of its aniconism in the ancient traditions of the northern Arabian tribes.[45] In light of these tribes' claim of kinship with the Jews, the parallel between the Nabateans' aversion to idols and the Jewish prohibition of graven images is unmistakable. Indeed, experts believe that the Nabatean and Jewish religions share the same ancient roots.[46]

This theory is reinforced by the story of Jacob's ladder in Genesis 28. Abraham's grandson Jacob used a stone for his pillow, and after seeing in a dream a stairway to heaven, he wrestled with an angel. After his mystical experience, he set up a standing stone and called that place Bethel, which means "house of God." The standing stones in Nabatean temples are called "betyls," and scholars have not been slow to see the connection between them and Jacob's holy place Bethel.[47]

While the Nabatean religion recognized a variety of gods and goddesses, it would be wrong to describe it as polytheistic. A better term is "henotheistic," referring to a religion that recognizes astral beings—demigods, demons, angels, and the like—all of which are subservient to a dominant god, whom the Nabateans called Dushara.

This might seem alien to Judaism, which we usually think of as strictly monotheistic. "Dushara," however, is not a divine name as such, explains John Healey, but a circumlocution which means "He who is of the Shara Mountains."[48] Likewise, the ancient Jews referred to the Almighty as "The One of Sinai." Like their brothers the Jews, the Nabateans prohibited the use of a proper name for God. Margaret Barker points out that in the older, Abrahamic Judaism (which would have been centered in Arabia), there were many names for God. The older Judaism was therefore similarly henotheistic.[49]

Healey calls such a religion "emergent monotheism."[50] Biblical scholars now believe that the Jews did not become explicitly monotheistic until this same crucial transitional period of the sixth century BC. The second section of the book of Isaiah was written during this period by a Jew exiled in Babylon or a Babylonian colony, and scholars cite chapter forty-four (verses six through eight) as the first unambiguous assertion of Jewish monotheism.

Because of the shared ancestry of the Jews and the northern Arabian tribes and because of the influx of Jews after the destruction of Jerusalem, Nabatean culture was deeply Abrahamic, and the Nabateans would have had a natural interest in a newborn king of neighboring Judea.

If we dig more deeply into the history and personalities of the Middle East in the sixth century BC, we shall discover another powerful cultural influence that answers the riddle of the Nabateans' sudden appearance and provides further evidence of the true identity of Matthew's wise men.

CHAPTER SIX

The Middle Eastern Melting Pot

When I retold the story of the Magi to some middle school students some time ago, one of them raised his hand and asked, "Why did they even care about some faraway king of the Jews?"

He was like the boy who declared that the emperor was wearing nothing at all. The middle school boy asked a question that very few have bothered to ask. "What would have motivated Persian magi to make such a journey?" Assuming, for the sake of argument, that they had seen some sort of portent in the night sky about a Jewish monarch, why would that necessarily prompt them to set out on a long journey to find him? Why would they care?

As we have seen, by the time of Christ's birth the Persian magi were a spent force. The Parthian king, Phraates IV, even if he retained any magian advisors, had no interest in a newborn king of the Jews. Neither would the Zoroastrian magi have had any particular interest in the Jews and their religion.

In the last chapter, however, I showed how the Nabateans had a shared ancestry with the Jews and deep roots in Abrahamic lore and culture. They would have been profoundly interested in a newborn Jewish king. When we get to know the Nabateans better we will see that they had even more motivations to seek the Christ child. To understand those motives we have to dig more deeply into their origins. The roots of their culture will reveal more of what they believed and therefore what was important to them and what drove them.

Desert Cosmopolitans

The key to understanding the Nabateans is to see their civilization as a melting pot. Aryeh Kasher observes that "the Nabateans succeeded in bringing other ethnic elements from among the previous permanent residents who lived in their vicinity on the edge of the desert into their tribal federation."[1] Evidence of this is the continued tolerance of the cults of various tribal gods within Nabatean society.[2] While they believed in one dominant God, they had room for various demigods. Therefore, in addition to tolerating the various tribal gods, during later periods the Nabateans were also open to Persian, Greek, and Roman religious ideas. As Philip Hammond, an archaeologist and Nabatean specialist, observes:

> Although situated well away from the major urban centers of her neighbors, Petra touched, and was touched by the cultural streams of the Hellenistic-Roman world. By the time of Aretas IV [late first century BC] and, undoubtedly much earlier, these streams were not seen to be "foreign," but part of the everyday culture of all peoples in the Mediterranean world.[3]

By the time of the birth of Christ, these "streams" had produced a diverse and multi-layered culture. We have examined the Arab and Jewish contributions, but the Persians, too, influenced Nabatean culture during the centuries in which the Neo-Babylonian and Persian empires dominated the region.[4] Kasher makes the point that Nabatean expansion was "due to Persian inspiration and permission, or at least Persian non-intervention."[5]

The Nabateans were connected to Persia by trade as well as by politics, their trade routes running north from Arabia into Persia and west to the port of Gaza.[6] Indeed, before the rise of Greece and Rome, the Nabateans' primary trading partners would have been the Persians. Aramaic was the international language of trade during the Persian period, so the Nabateans' use of Aramaic also indicates a strong Persian influence.[7]

Stephanie Dalley provides a glimpse into the Babylonian court at the time of the conquest of Jerusalem: "The court of Nebuchadnezzar was famous for its cosmopolitan society. Phoenicians, Syrians, Elamites, and Egyptians rubbed shoulders with Ionians and Israelites, feasting together and conversing in Aramaic. Well-educated members of the nobility and well-travelled professional mercenaries shared experiences and ideas."[8]

Why does this matter? Because along with the existing Arab tribes and the Jewish immigrants, the Babylonian presence contributed to the cosmopolitan character of the Nabatean culture. The Jewish refugees were part of this melting-pot Babylonian society, but they were also free to settle elsewhere. Dalley notes that "not all deportees stayed at the royal court, nor even in Babylon. Many of them made a new life in the enclaves of foreigners frequently attached to other cities."[9]

One of the places where émigré Jews, Arabians, and Babylonians mixed was the northern Arabian oasis of Tayma, a city important for our story because of the intriguing character who settled there, a man who embodied the blend of Babylonian and Jewish influences—the last king of the Babylonians, Nabonidus.

Fig. 7 Photo showing a relief carving of King Nabonidus at Sela. *Courtesy of Wikimedia Commons.*

Nabonidus the Odd

In 1994, in the ancient Edomite hill fort of Sela, just north of Petra, archaeologists discovered a relief carving of a figure in a long Babylonian royal robe and pointed cap. The figure holds a scepter in his right hand, and his left is raised toward a crescent moon, a winged sun, and a seven-pointed star representing the planet Venus. Most scholars believe the carving portrays Nabonidus, the last king of the Neo-Babylonian Empire, who died in 539 BC.[10]

While many kings of antiquity were dubbed "the Great," Nabonidus might well be called "the Odd."[11] Hyper-religious, he was devoted
to the Babylonian moon god Sin—an archaic devotion by then—of
which his mother was a priestess.[12] The carving at Sela provides
archaeological evidence for Nabonidus's invasion of northern Arabia
in 553–552 BC.[13] He bolstered his conquest of the territory by building a network of forts[14] before going on to establish a series of Babylonian colonies in northern Arabia.[15]

Instead of returning to Babylon after his conquest, Nabonidus
took the unusual step of establishing an alternative capital in Tayma,[16]
believing that Sin had commanded him to reside there.[17] He stayed in
that city, in the heart of what would become Nabatean territory, for
ten years, building palaces and temples and organizing a new admin-
istration for the area.[18] Noting that "the city [of Tayma] enjoyed a
high degree of civilization at that time, with its religious life largely
colored by Babylonian influence," the historian Raymond Dougherty
concluded that "Arabia seems to have been intimately connected with
Babylonia in the 6th century B. C."[19]

The sophisticated atmosphere of Nebuchadnezzar's court must
have been replicated in Tayma during the reign of Nabonidus. Indeed,
"[t]emples decorated with Egyptian statues, South Arabian inscriptions, and carvings with Mesopotamian motifs" recently excavated
there "attest to Tayma's cosmopolitan nature."[20]

Tayma was the hub of the lucrative trans-Arabian trading routes,
and its commercial atmosphere, supported by the king himself, helps to
explain the sudden appearance of the Nabateans. But Nabonidus had
more than "mercantile and political" reasons for his sojourn in Tayma,
says the Biblical scholar Alan Millard. He had religious reasons as well.[21]

Nabonidus, Friend of Jews

Nabonidus had a special relationship with the Jews. Tayma was
the oldest colony of Jews in Arabia, and at the time of Nabonidus's

stay there, it was a haven for expatriate Jews,[22] many of whom, along with native Babylonian Jews, served as soldiers.[23]

The more we learn more about Nabonidus, the more intriguing are his links with the Jews. One of the Dead Sea Scrolls, discovered just across the border from what was Nabatean territory, recounts how Nabonidus went to Tayma after being afflicted with terrible boils. After his healing by a Jewish exorcist, he issued a proclamation in the name of the "most High God."[24] One author makes a strong case that the book of Job was written in Tayma during the reign of Nabonidus,[25] while André Lemaire even suggests that portions of the Old Testament book of Isaiah might have originated among the Jewish exiles in Tayma.[26]

Nabonidus considered it his mission to revitalize the god Sin's worship, which had three ancient centers. The first two were the cities of Ur and Harran. The third was Tayma.[27] According to the Nabonidus Cylinders,[28] the king, in obedience to Sin, rebuilt the ancient shrines to the moon god in Harran, appointed his daughter priestess at the shrine to Sin in Ur, and removed himself from Babylon to Tayma for ten years.[29] Thus, in an extraordinary way, the Babylonian and Jewish influences meet. The book of Genesis records that the patriarch Abraham came from Ur and Harran,[30] and Tayma was the name of one of the sons of Abraham's son Ishmael.[31]

Because of Abraham's origins at Ur and Harran, some scholars believe the Jewish religion had its origins in the worship of the moon god Sin.[32] Is it a coincidence that the ancient centers of worship for the Babylonian moon god were located at Ur, Harran, and Tayma? Had Nabonidus met Jewish exiles in Babylon, learned about their ancestor's roots in Ur, Harran, and Tayma, and concluded that the Jews' true roots were in his own Mesopotamian homeland?

Centuries earlier, during the time of Abraham, the god Sin was called En-zu, or "Lord of Wisdom." En-zu was also the "Father of All Gods" and the "Creator of All Things."[33] Did Nabonidus, seeing similarities between Sin and the Jewish Father-Creator God, decide that the Jews' noble religion and the ancient Babylonian worship of

En-zu (Sin) could be merged to produce a unified religion?[34] Is that why he was so intent on reviving the worship of Sin? The Harran inscriptions indicate that during his ten years away from Babylon, Nabonidus also stayed in other Arabian towns.[35] Was this an attempt to spread his blend of Abrahamic-Babylonian religion?

The religious developments in the sixth century BC offer more intriguing clues. John Healey observes that in the time of Nabonidus, the god Marduk was becoming preeminent among the Babylonian gods, a sign of "emergent monotheism."[36] Paul-Alain Beaulieu thinks King Nabonidus's attempts to promote the moon god as the supreme deity were essentially henotheistic.[37] Also emerging at this time was Zoroastrianism, monotheistic and forbidding graven images. Herodotus observed that the Persians "have no images of the gods, nor altars nor temples."[38] Considering all these influences, André Lemaire identifies the reign of Nabonidus as the time when monotheism emerged from a blending of Babylonian-Zoroastrian and Jewish traditions and theology.[39]

The Nabateans were also influenced by Greek philosophy. Cicero records that the famed philosophers Pythagoras (d. 495 BC) and Democritus (d. 370 BC) visited the magi in Arabia.[40] By the time of Christ's birth, Greek and Roman culture had also been absorbed by the Nabateans. King Aretas III (d. 62 BC) titled himself Philhellen, "Friend of the Greeks," and the archaeological evidence indicates the adoption of Greek and Roman religion and philosophy as well as architecture and technology.

The melting pot of Nabatean culture is more than merely interesting. It is the essential background for the discovery of the true identity of the wise men who visited Bethlehem.

The Nabatean Magi

The Nabatean connection with Matthew's story of the Magi is important for several reasons. First, as neighbors, the Nabateans would have had a political and economic interest in who was on the Judean throne.

Fig. 8 Photo showing the tomb of Darius. *Courtesy of Wikimedia Commons.*

Second, because of their ancestral links and similarities to Abrahamic Judaism and the large numbers of Jewish immigrants, the Nabateans would have had a historical, religious, and cultural interest in the Jewish monarchy.

Third, if the culture of the Nabateans was a blend of Arabian, Abrahamic, Babylonian, and Greek elements, then the religion must also have reflected this blend, which is what the archaeological evidence reveals.[41] And if their religion reflected this blend, then their religious leaders—the priests and sages we might call the Nabatean magi—must have reflected it as well. If that is true, then the other pieces of the puzzle fall into place.

It sounds plausible, but because there is no written history of the Nabateans, the existence of magi in Petra or Tayma remains speculation.

Or does it? Is there further evidence for the existence of magi in the region of Nabatea?

The carved figure in Sela that scholars have identified as King Nabonidus holds a mysterious clue. It is not clear whether the ancient structure at Sela was only a fort. There are signs that it might also have been a religious shrine.[42] As the carved figure is portrayed with astral signs, including the crescent moon, the sign of the god Sin; Venus, a star that often stood for Zoroaster; and the winged sun, which is a symbol of the Zoroastrian god Ahura Mazda, might the mysterious figure be a magian priest from Babylon?

The Babylonian influence on the Nabateans was not merely political, military, and economic. Nabonidus was an especially religious monarch. Sin was also associated with astrology,[43] and the worship of Sin involved charting the lunar cycles to predict the future. The portrayals of Nabonidus show him gazing up at the Zoroastrian astral symbols. Was Nabonidus not only an eccentric king but a magian, stargazing priest?

The moon god Sin (En-zu) was also the Lord of Wisdom.[44] It would certainly be consistent with what we know of the magi and Nabonidus to conclude that this king had wise men and astrologers with him at his court in exile at Tayma.

These are reasonable speculations, but there is also archaeological evidence for Babylonian magi in Arabia. The tombs and temples in Petra echo the earlier royal tombs in Persia, and a carved head of a priest was uncovered in Petra showing the same high headgear and Babylonian-style facial hair that are found in the carvings of King Nabonidus and in the wall carvings of Persian priests in Persopolis.

But there are other important historical events that prove the Babylonian magi were present in Arabia.

In 539 BC Nabonidus's Neo-Babylonian kingdom fell to Cyrus the Great. As we saw in chapter four, seventeen years later Darius took the Persian throne, suppressing the magi after they supported the usurper Gaumata.

As the Jews had fled from Nebuchadnezzar into Arabia in 586 BC, the magi fled from Darius into northern Arabia some sixty years later.[45] And as the Jews found refuge in the existing Jewish colonies, so the magian refugees would have found refuge in Petra, Tayma, and the other Babylonian colonies of Arabia.

Over the years, the Persian magi were dispersed for other reasons as well. They went into Persian colonies as missionaries.[46] The Roman historian Pliny identifies Arabia as one of the areas where the expatriate magi were to be found,[47] and as early as the seventeenth century scholars of Arabian history noted that the magi were to be found in Arabia as well as Persia.[48] The patristics scholar Jean Daniélou agreed: "We know that at the beginning of the Christian era there were Iranian magi all over the Middle East, especially in Syria."[49]

The Persian magi, skilled astrologers and priests, were also the most brilliant mathematicians, court administrators, and teachers. Pythagoras and Democritus learned from them, and the astronomer Michael Molnar calls them "the scientists of their day."[50] The Persian wise men would have brought all these gifts to the burgeoning Nabatean nation, while the Jewish refugees from Jerusalem's collapse brought architectural know-how and mercantile and administrative skills. Meanwhile the Jewish priests who fled in the seventh century contributed their own ancient traditions and wisdom to the religious scene.

By the time of the birth of Christ, the influence of the magi had faded in Persia. They still existed, but as we have seen, they had no real motive to make a journey to find a Jewish king. The Nabatean magi, on the other hand, had deep roots in Abrahamic religion, had absorbed later Jewish cultural influences, were steeped in the magian lore of Babylon, and, by the time of Christ's birth, had absorbed elements of Greek religion and philosophy. It was natural that such men should have a deep interest in a newborn king of the Jews.

This intriguing mix of Babylonian and Jewish religion in northern Arabia in the sixth century also influenced the writings of the Jewish prophets. Filled with hope of a savior king, they prophesied the coming of a world messiah.

The astounding discovery of the Dead Sea Scrolls in 1946 established new links between the ancient Jewish prophecies and the Nabateans. The scrolls shed light on the period leading up to the birth of Christ and provide more evidence in the quest for the true identity of Matthew's wise men.

Prophecies or Predictions?

From time immemorial, human beings have turned for guidance to shamans, witches, and wise men. Hoping to glimpse the future, these soothsayers have altered their consciousness through drugs, meditation, or whipping themselves into a religious frenzy. They have attempted to read the future in stars, magical cards, crystal balls, tea leaves, the entrails of animals, prophecies, and the palm of your hand.

Christians have often approached Biblical prophecies with this same fascination, treating the Old Testament prophets as seers with a supernatural view into the future.[1] It would be easy to understand Matthew's treatment of prophecy in this way. Because he frequently notes the fulfillment of prophecy, we might suppose that he viewed the Old Testament as a treasure chest of mystical prognostications.

Explaining the Virgin Birth, for example, he writes, "All this took place to fulfill what the Lord had said through the prophet" (Matthew 1:22), and he goes on to quote the Old Testament prophet Isaiah, "Behold a virgin shall conceive and bear a son, and they shall call his name Emmanuel" (Isaiah 7:14).

Skeptical critics conclude that Matthew simply made up the story of the Virgin Birth to fit Isaiah's prophecy, hoping to convince his readers that since the prophet's forecast had been supernaturally fulfilled, Jesus must have been the long-awaited Messiah—the Son of God.[2] This understanding of Matthew's gospel and the role of prophecy in the Bible and Jewish tradition, however, is too simplistic.

It is true that Matthew thinks the birth, life, and death of Jesus fulfill Old Testament prophecies, but his approach is far more subtle than critics suppose. With a more nuanced understanding of how prophecy is "fulfilled" in the gospel, we can replace this superstitious fortune-telling approach with a more natural and commonsense explanation.

Fulfillment or Recapitulation?

Matthew does identify certain events in the gospel as fulfillments of specific Old Testament prophecies, but that is not his main concern. He seeds the gospel with these pointers—"thus it was written in order that the prophecy might be fulfilled"—to lead his reader to a wider understanding of how God works in the world and a deeper understanding of the story of Jesus Christ.

Instead of focusing on particular prophecies that come true in Matthew's gospel, we should see the whole gospel as a fulfillment of the Old Testament.[3] Virtually every story in Matthew's gospel echoes some Old Testament event or character. The infant Jesus' deliverance from Herod's murderous designs is like the delivery of the child Moses from the evil plans of Pharaoh. Preaching the Sermon on the Mount, Jesus is a second Moses, who from the mountain delivered the Ten Commandments. The multiplication of the loaves and fishes echoes

Moses' feeding of the people of Israel with manna in the wilderness. John the Baptist is a second Elijah.

In practically every chapter of Matthew's gospel the quick-eyed student of the Bible will spot a reference of some kind to the Old Testament. The evangelist quotes Jesus himself, who says to his disciples, "Do not think that I have come to abolish the Law or the Prophets; I have not come to abolish them but to fulfill them" (Matthew 5:17). It is Matthew's gospel in particular that bears out Augustine's observation that "the New Testament is hidden in the Old, and the Old Testament is made manifest in the New."[4]

The second-century Christian theologian Irenaeus called this kind of fulfillment "recapitulation."[5] Indeed, it was not only the Old Testament that was fulfilled in Jesus Christ's life, death, and resurrection but all of human history. In the larger Christian view, the whole of creation is a story, of which the Old Testament prophecies are only a piece. The recapitulation of the human story in Christ represents a more intriguing and theologically compelling understanding of prophecy than simply looking at one event and deciding that it supernaturally "fulfilled" a particular prophecy in the Old Testament.

To understand an Old Testament prophecy, we need to understand its context and motivation. In our particular quest to identify the Magi, we will see how the Old Testament prophecies connect Matthew's wise men to the Nabatean magi of northern Arabia.

Prophecies or Predictions?

The best approach to a possibly supernatural phenomenon is a simple one. We exercise a careful skepticism, and we always look for the natural explanation first. We don't exclude the possibility of the supernatural, but a reasonable method means we look for the ordinary answer before we propose a supernatural cause.

This principle applies to prophecy as it does to more unusual supernatural phenomena. We admit that unexplained insights into the future might occur. A person with an unusual psychic gift might be able to glimpse the future, and God might enlighten a person to see the future through dreams, visions, or inner locutions. First, however, we should consider the more prosaic possibility that the visionary is deluded, emotionally unstable, or mentally ill. While we admit that prophesying the future is possible, we exercise common sense and suggest that what many believe are prophecies may simply be predictions.

With hindsight, it is easy to see prophecies as supernatural glimpses into the future. If a prophecy has "come true," it is tempting to read into it a supernatural power to foretell the future—tempting, but usually not necessary. So, for example, in Matthew 24:1–8, Jesus forecasts the destruction of the temple in Jerusalem. Jesus died in AD 33, and the temple was indeed destroyed, along with the whole city of Jerusalem, thirty-seven years later. It would seem that Jesus had supernatural foresight.

He could well have had supernatural foresight, but that was not required to forecast disaster for the Jews. For decades they had been fighting with one another, with their Greek overlords, and then with the Romans. Violent rebellions flared up constantly and were put down with typical Roman cruelty. Jesus understood the Jews. He understood the Romans. He understood the political situation. Knowing the stubbornness of the Jews and the ruthlessness of the Romans, it wouldn't have taken much for him to predict the eventual destruction of Jerusalem.[6]

When we understand the historical context at the time of the Old Testament prophecies, we will see that most often they are predictions, not supernatural glimpses into the future. In other words, they are like a weather report—a logical prediction of what might happen based on data, common sense, and the circumstances at the time of writing.

Looking for the Lord

The Old Testament passages that seem to prophesy the visitation of the Magi must be put into the larger religious and cultural context of their time. The first prophecy that Christians have understood as foretelling the visitation of the Magi is found in the book of Numbers, during the time when Moses was leading the Israelites through the desert. A non-Jewish seer and shaman named Balaam, who comes "from the East," is asked to cast a spell against the Israelites by Balak, the king of Moab. But having been visited by an angel, Balaam instead confers a triple blessing upon the Israelites, telling the vexed Balak, "I see him, but not now; I behold him, but not near: a star shall come out of Jacob, and a scepter shall rise out of Israel..." (Numbers 24:17).

From antiquity, students of Scripture have spent a good bit of time and effort elaborating the parallels between the stories of Balaam and of the Magi.[7] Raymond Brown has connected the dots, calling Balaam a kind of "magus" from the East and positing that Matthew constructed his story to show how the visit of the Magi fulfilled Balaam's prophecy.[8]

The difficulty with Brown's hypothesis is that there are as many dissimilarities between the Magi story and the Balaam story as there are similarities. We can assume that Matthew knew the story of Balaam and his prophecy that "a star shall come out of Jacob," but it is clear that Balaam's "star" refers to a coming ruler of the Israelites who will vanquish their enemies. If Matthew were constructing the Magi story to line up with Balaam's prophecy, he didn't do a very good job. It's more likely that Matthew knew of the visit of the Nabatean Magi to Bethlehem and saw it as a general fulfillment of the Balaam tale.

The prophecy of Balaam, however, is interesting for another reason. It clearly predicts the coming of a mighty ruler or savior. The expectation of a Messiah was commonplace throughout the ancient world. The Essenes—a first-century Jewish sect at Qumran—interpreted Balaam's words as a Messianic prophecy,[9] and the early Christians discerned in it an aspect of the Zoroastrian religion, which looked forward to the advent of a Messiah who would be born of a virgin, "raise the dead and crush the forces of evil."[10]

This belief in a world savior was "one of the most widely popular premises of the Persian religion, and found ready acceptance wherever people longed for redemption."[11] The Roman historians Suetonius (d. AD 140) and Tacitus (d. AD 117) were aware of the prophecy of Balaam and of the widely held belief that a great world ruler would arise from among the Jews.[12] Furthermore, early Christians read these lines from the Fourth Eclogue of the Roman poet Virgil (d. 19 BC) and could not help but conclude that the whole world was looking for a Messiah:

> Now is come the last age of the Cumaean prophecy:
> The great cycle of periods is born anew.
> Now returns the Maid, returns the reign of Saturn:
> Now from high heaven a new generation comes down.
> Yet do thou at that boy's birth,
> In whom the iron race shall begin to cease,
> And the golden to arise over all the world....[13]

The prophecies of a Messiah had been present within Jewish tradition for much longer. At first they were hints and guesses, but then, at the same time that the Nabateans began to emerge in Arabia, they came into sharper focus. As the northern Arabian tribes absorbed the Jews and Babylonians, the Messianic hopes from both the Zoroastrian and Jewish traditions cross-fertilized each other, and out of this blend of wisdom and tradition came some of the writings of the Jewish Old Testament.

Jewish Babylonian Wisdom

One strand of Old Testament writings with roots in this melting-pot culture is the "wisdom literature": the ancient proverbs, poems, and drama through which practical and spiritual wisdom was passed down among the Jews. Wisdom literature, which was popular in Babylon, found its way into the Old Testament in the books of Job, the Psalms, the Song of Songs, Wisdom, Ecclesiastes, Proverbs, and Sirach, showing the influence of the Babylonians on Jewish culture in Arabia. Tony Maalouf has shown that the book of Job, for example, is rooted in the experience and literature of the tribes of northern Arabia,[14] and scholars suggest it dates from the sixth century BC, the crucial period in which the foundations of the Nabatean culture were being established.[15]

The poetry of the Babylonian-influenced wisdom literature indicates the existence of a school of Jewish wise men or prophets active in Arabia in the sixth century BC and beyond. Emerging from the school of wise men were the prophets who carried on the wisdom traditions of the Jews. The prophets were, if you like, Jewish magi. Seers and oracles, they served as influential court advisors. It is in their writings that we have the most important texts about the wise men, the most astounding of which are found in the second part of the book of Isaiah.

Isaiah in Arabia

Biblical scholars believe the first thirty-nine chapters of the book of Isaiah were mostly written by the prophet Isaiah in Judea in the eighth century BC.[16] In the nineteenth century, however, scholars came to the conclusion that the second part of the book of Isaiah was composed later by other prophets in the "school of Isaiah." From historical references, they have concluded that so-called "Second Isaiah" was composed after the conquest of Jerusalem in 586 BC by a member of the Jewish community in exile.[17] Lemaire suggests that the prophet of Second Isaiah may have settled in the city of Tayma during Nabonidus's reign,[18] where there might have been a school of prophets or wise men.

Lemaire's insight offers an intriguing clue to the origins of Isaiah's prophecies and their connection with the Nabateans. If Second Isaiah originated among the exiled Jews in Arabia, the prophecies are charged with meaning.

Second Isaiah, which begins with chapter forty, contains some of the most beautiful and inspiring passages in the entire Bible. God will come to redeem his people, the prophet says. He will rescue them from the nations and bring them home as a shepherd gathers his flock. He will defeat their enemies and reward them with justice.

Chapters forty to forty-four are filled with references to the "wilderness" and "coastlands." God will "make a straight way in the desert" (Isaiah 40:3–5). The water technology of the Nabateans, which transforms the desert, is evoked: "I will open up rivers on the bare heights, and fountains in the broad valleys; I will turn the wilderness into a marshland, and the dry ground into springs of water. In the wilderness I will plant the cedar, acacia, myrtle, and olive" (Isaiah 41:18–19). The prophet calls to the coastlands for silence, and they see and are afraid (Isaiah 41:1–5). These references to the long coastlines and desert wilderness sound as though the prophet is writing from Arabia, not the lush river valley of Babylon.

Apart from these suggestions of a general Arabian setting, two important passages in Second Isaiah provide a link to the Nabateans. In chapter forty-two, the prophet looks forward to a servant of the Lord who will bring justice to the nations. The servant will be a great warrior who rescues those in prison and restores those who are refugees. Verse twenty-two describes a people like the refugees from the destruction of Jerusalem: "plundered and despoiled, all of them trapped in holes, hidden away in prisons. They are taken as plunder, with no one to rescue them."

The original Isaiah had recognized Arabia, and the city of Tayma in particular, as a refuge for those escaping war and persecution. "In the thicket in the steppe [northern Arabia] you will spend the night, caravans of Dedanites.[19] Meet the thirsty, bring them water, inhabitants of the land of Tayma, greet the fugitives with bread. For they have fled from the sword, from the drawn sword, from the taut bow, from the thick of battle" (Isaiah 21:13–15).

Second Isaiah says the exiles will rejoice at the coming of their savior and specifies that they have taken refuge in the northern Arabian desert. In 42:11, the prophet cries, "Let the wilderness and its cities cry out, the villages where Kedar dwells; let the inhabitants of Sela exult, and shout from the top of the mountains." Kedar was one of the tribes of northern Arabia that merged with the Nabateans, and Sela we have already encountered—it is the hilltop fortress just a few miles north of Petra where the carving of King Nabonidus was discovered.

The forty-second chapter of Isaiah is replete with condemnations of idol worship. The prophet echoes the Lord saying, "I am the Lord, Lord is my name; my glory I give to no other, nor my praise to idols" (Isaiah 42:8). In verse seventeen, idol worshippers are condemned: "They shall be turned back in utter shame, who trust in idols; who say to molten images, 'You are our gods.'"

Chapter forty-four also contains an extended condemnation of idols and idol worshippers and pronounces a clear assertion of monotheism: "Is there any God but me? There is no other Rock, I know of none!" (Isaiah 44:8).

The condemnation of idol worship fits perfectly with what we know of the Nabatean religion, with its rejection of graven images. The reference to God as the "Rock" reflects the aniconic religion of the Nabateans with their monolithic representations of deities, and the assertion of monotheism fits with the "emergent monotheism" that historians have observed in the sixth century BC.[20]

Nabateans of the Nations

The sixtieth chapter of Isaiah contains the most famous prophecy of the wise men. Scholars believe that by the time these prophecies were written, some Jews had returned to Jerusalem and that the author of this passage is encouraging the people by looking forward with joy to the day when all the Jews who have been scattered will return to the Holy City. Indeed, in this vision, all the nations of the world will make their way to Jerusalem to rebuild the city and pay homage. In chapter fifty-six the prophet explains how the foreigners will come to worship the Jewish God. They will be welcome, their prayers and offerings accepted, when "my house shall be called a house of prayer for all peoples" (Isaiah 56:7).

It is the Jews of North Arabia—the land of the Nabateans—who will lead the way. The prophet says to the Jews:

> Raise your eyes and look about;
> they all gather and come to you—
> Your sons from afar,
> your daughters in the arms of their nurses.
> Then you shall see and be radiant,
> your heart shall throb and overflow.
> For the riches of the sea shall be poured out before you,
> the wealth of nations shall come to you.
> Caravans of camels shall cover you,
> dromedaries of Midian and Ephah;
> All from Sheba shall come
> bearing gold and frankincense,
> and heralding the praises of the Lord.
> All the flocks of Kedar shall be gathered for you,
> the rams of Nebaioth shall serve your needs;
> They will be acceptable offerings on my altar,
> and I will glorify my glorious house (Isaiah 60:4–7).

Who will lead the nations to worship the Lord? It is the Jews and their ancient kinsmen who had settled in Arabia. "Ephah" is the son of Midian, one of Abraham's sons (Genesis 25:4). Ephah gives his name to another northern Arabian tribe, famous for using camel caravans for the frankincense trade.[21] "Sheba" refers to Jews from Yemen or the kingdom of Saba in southern Arabia,[22] while the "flocks of Kedar" refer to the northern Arabian tribe of Qedarites who merged with the Nabateans.[23] The "Nebaioth," as we saw in chapter five, are the tribe many believe are the ancestors of the Nabateans.

These prophecies from Isaiah are important not because they provide an occult, supernatural glimpse into the future, but because they reveal a genuine hope and a commonsense prediction by an author writing in the tradition of Isaiah in the sixth century BC. Writing in Arabia for exiled Jews, he sees God's hand at work. Despite the trauma and tragedy of exile, the faith has been kept alive, and from the melting pot of the emerging Nabatean civilization he can see that something good will come. He can see that the exile of Jews in Arabia has been a way to reconcile with their ancient kinsmen—the tribes who shared their Abrahamic ancestry.

The prophet can see that the Jewish faith was renewed as it returned to its Abrahamic roots. It also expanded as it accepted salutary Babylonian influences. From this dynamic blend, the prophet predicts that the nations of the world, with whom the nascent Nabateans are trading, will one day see the light and come to Jerusalem to pay homage to the Messiah, and wise rulers from this civilization will lead the way.

The Nabateans and the Dead Sea Scrolls

A few centuries later the story of the Isaian prophecies becomes even more interesting. The prophecies we have considered were probably written in the sixth century BC among the exiled Jews in Neo-Babylonian settlements in northern Arabia, such as Rechem (Petra), Tayma, or Sela, and the Jews of northern Arabia would have copied and preserved them over the centuries. The discovery in 1947 of the Dead Sea Scrolls in the caves of Qumran—on the edge of Nabatean territory, a short distance from Sela and Petra—confirms the care with which these Arabian Jews preserved their sacred writings.

At the time of Christ's birth, Qumran was occupied by the Essenes, a Jewish monastic community known for their asceticism and messianic expectations, who were probably responsible for maintaining the extensive and already ancient library of the Hebrew Scriptures, copied on papyrus scrolls and stored in pottery jars in cave libraries. One of the best preserved of these is the Great Isaiah scroll. A virtually complete copy of the book of Isaiah, it may date to 330

BC,[24] just two hundred years after the prophecies were first composed and at least a century before the establishment of the Essene community. We know that the prophecies of Isaiah were important to the exiled Jews not only because they preserved the scrolls but also because archaeologists have discovered at Qumran notes and commentaries on Isaiah's writings.

The production of the Great Isaiah scroll and these commentaries in the same area of northwest Arabia and at the same time as the growth of the Nabatean culture would support Lemaire's suggestion that the Isaian prophecies originated in Tayma, Petra, or one of the other emerging Nabatean colonies where exiled Jews had settled.

Even more intriguing, the religious community at Qumran had a fascination with astrology. The text 4Q186 of the Dead Sea Scrolls describes the appearance of a person and his spiritual makeup according to his astrological chart. "His spirit has six parts in the house of light and three parts in the house of darkness. He will be born under the haunch of Taurus and his sign is the bull."[25] It is possible that the community who left us the Dead Sea Scrolls also used this astrological method to determine the appearance of the world savior who was to come.[26]

What conclusion can we draw from this archaeological and textual evidence? The Nabatean civilization developed out of the melting pot of northern Arabian tribes, exiled Jews, and Neo-Babylonians. The prophecies of Isaiah originated in the Nabatean territory, where they were treasured and preserved. Second Isaiah spoke of a coming savior who would bring justice and open the way for the whole world to worship the one true God, and the Nabatean Jews would be the ones who led the way.

It could well be that Nabatean magi—Jewish wise men influenced by Neo-Babylonian religion—were the original authors of Second Isaiah. Certainly the Nabatean wise men at the time of Christ's birth must have known of Isaiah's prophecies. The Essenes of Qumran, who preserved the prophecies of Isaiah and practiced astrology, were on the Nabateans' doorstep. Rabbis and other religious teachers of the time maintained libraries and formed schools of their followers. Was there a college of Nabatean wise men who cultivated a blend of Jewish wisdom, Babylonian lore, and Greek learning? If so, they must have known when they saw the signs in the night sky and set out on their journey to Jerusalem that they were playing a part in a larger, more ancient, and important cosmic drama.

The Biblical prophecies show God's work in the world always intersecting with human machinations, and the coming of Jesus Christ is no exception. The Nabateans, sharing roots with the exiled Jews, Neo-Babylonians, and Greeks, discovered their connection with a major player in the drama of Christ's birth—the king of the Jews, Herod the Great.

CHAPTER EIGHT

The Herod Connection

Herod the Great (d. 4 BC) has been described as a "good king but a bad man." Famous for being paranoid, lustful, greedy, and murderously vindictive, he was also a shrewd tactician, a master builder, a cunning political operator, and, most notably, a survivor in the political and military maelstrom of the first years of the Roman Empire.

Herod is integral to the story of the wise men because it was to his court that they first came looking for the newborn king of the Jews. Troubled by their visit, he met with them secretly and slyly told them, "Go and search diligently for the child, and when you have found him, bring me word, that I too may come and worship him" (Matthew 2:8).

The Magi's visit to Herod's court is strong evidence that they were from Nabatea, not Persia-Parthia, and this scenario fits precisely with Herod's personal story and the politics of the time. To see how the pieces of the puzzle fit together we need to examine more closely the complex history of the Middle East in the second half of the first century BC.

The Blossoming of the Nabateans

The Nabatean civilization emerged from the melting pot of the northern Arabian tribes, Jews, and Neo-Babylonians in the mid-sixth century BC. Over the next 250 years, the Nabateans remained obscure, but as Jane Taylor points out,

> they were clearly already in a process of metamorphosis [from a nomadic to a settled civilization] for they had acquired possessions that were not easily transported in a nomadic life. Such immovables needed protection, and for this they must have had at least a general concept of central organization. They had, we are told, a special rock (*petra*), which was virtually impregnable since it had only one path to the top, and there they stored their most valuable possessions.[1]

The first mention of the Nabateans in the historical record comes toward the end of the fourth century BC, when they defended themselves from the Greeks. After the death of Alexander the Great in 323 BC, his empire was torn apart in a power struggle. One of his generals, Antigonus the One-Eyed, attempted to gain control, and around 312 BC, as he moved south through Syria, Antigonus instructed his general Athenaeus to attack the Nabateans. Their strategic victory over the Greeks established them as a major force in the region. Taylor observes, "The pragmatism and diplomacy they had displayed—for the first time to the 'civilized' world—were repeated in different ways, and developed, over the following centuries in their relationships with their neighbors."[2]

During the next few centuries, the Nabateans minded their own business, more concerned about developing trade than about becoming a political or military power. Then in the century before the birth of Jesus Christ, when they had settled in Petra and established a monarchy, their history starts to come into political and cultural focus. The Jewish historian Josephus records that when the Hasmonean king of Judea, Alexander Jannaeus (d. 76 BC), besieged the coastal town of Gaza, the citizens of the city expected help from the Nabatean king, Aretas II (d. 96 BC).[3] A few decades later Aretas III (d. 62 BC)—known as "Philhellen," or friend of the Greeks—expanded the Nabatean kingdom, building Greek-style temples and tombs in Petra and raising the level of sophistication of Nabatean culture.[4]

As the Greek empire crumbled, the wealthy Nabateans became more prominent. Dominating the Arabian trade routes and southern Judea, they came into conflict with the rising power of Rome.[5] It was precisely at this time that the Nabateans became increasingly involved in political events, giving them a reason to be very interested in a newborn king of the Jews.

The Hornet's Nest of the Middle East

The Middle East in the first century BC was a hornet's nest of rival monarchies and civil wars. It can be difficult to keep them straight, but the shifting relationships and political maneuverings provide more evidence that Nabatea was the home base of the wise men.

The Hasmoneans were a violent and unstable dynasty of Jews who ruled Judea, first under the auspices of the Greeks and then for a time on their own. In the decades leading up to the birth of Jesus, the remaining members of the Hasmonean dynasty clung to power while eyeing nervously the rising power of Rome and the equally daunting power of Parthia to the northeast.

Meanwhile, because the Nabateans needed access across southern Judea to the port of Gaza, their conflicts with the Hasmoneans simmered. The Roman general Pompey took advantage of the quarrel and advanced against both Jerusalem and Petra. His army was humiliated by the Nabateans, and the Nabatean king Aretas III established with the Romans what David Tschanz calls "a working accommodation with a high degree of ambivalence."[6]

Aretas III, however, was hedging his bets. When civil war broke out between Pompey and Julius Caesar, he sent soldiers to fight with Pompey in 48 BC, but a year later his soldiers fought with Julius Caesar. Aretas also had to consider whether his real allies might be the Parthians, who, having invaded Syria in 42 BC, moved south to knock out the Romans' vassal in Judea, the Hasmonean king Hyrcanus II. To keep the peace, the Parthians installed Hyrcanus's nephew Antigonus as king.

Herod the Great steps onto the stage at this point. He and his brother Phasael had been given positions of power in Judea during the reign of Hyrcanus II. Shrewdly building a power base and cultivating the favor of the Romans, they found their hopes dashed when the Parthians swept south and put Antigonus on the throne. The Parthians captured Phasael, who eventually committed suicide, while Herod escaped to Petra. King Aretas III's Nabatean successor, Malichus, did not welcome Herod, however, so he fled to Rome[7]—a wise move, for within two years the Romans had driven the Parthians out of Syria and Judea. The Judean throne was now vacant, and in 40 BC the emperor-to-be, Octavian, had the senate appoint Herod King of the Jews.[8]

The Plot Thickens

In order to appreciate the connection between Herod and Matthew's wise men, we must understand not only the complex political maneuverings in the decades before the birth of Christ but also Herod's family background. His father was an Idumean. Descended from the Edomites, the Idumeans had converted to Judaism under the reign of the Hasmonean king John Hyrcanus in 126 BC[9] and were therefore considered a kind of Jewish subset.[10]

Herod's father, Antipater, was the power behind the throne in the Hasmonean court of Hyrcanus II (d. 30 BC). Married to a Nabatean princess named Cypros, Antipater had five children: Phasael, Herod, Joseph, Pheroras, and Salome. When two Hasmonean rivals to the throne were feuding, Antipater sent Cypros and the children home to Petra for safety. The young Herod, therefore, was the son of a Nabatean princess and brought up at the court of the Nabatean royal family.[11]

Rewarded for having sided with Caesar against Pompey by being named chief minister of Judea, Antipater appointed his sons Herod and Phasael as governors of Judea and Galilee. During this time Antipater continued to enjoy excellent relations with his Nabatean relatives, receiving military support from the Nabatean king on several occasions.[12]

Antony and Cleopatra

When Herod was appointed king of Judea by Octavian in 40 BC, the political situation in the Middle East became even more complicated. In 38 BC, while Herod was busy crushing his enemies to consolidate his hold on the Judean throne, Mark Antony and Cleopatra of Egypt formed their famous alliance.

Mark Antony was master of the eastern part of the Roman Empire, while Octavian was ruler of the west. Herod was sworn to be the loyal vassal to Rome, but in the chain of command his superior was Antony, not Octavian. Cleopatra, meanwhile, intent on restoring Egypt's greatness, wanted to remove both Herod and the Nabatean king Malichus and take over the Judean and Nabatean territories.

In 32 BC, as Cleopatra whispered in Antony's ear to give her Judea, Antony and Octavian prepared for war against each other.

Herod was obliged to send troops to support Antony, but this put him in a tight spot. Should Octavian win and should Herod seem to have supported the traitor Antony, Octavian might depose or kill him. Should Antony win while Herod supported Octavian, Antony would have a perfect excuse to depose Herod and give his kingdom to Cleopatra.[13]

Herod found a way out. He attacked the Nabateans. The historian Aryeh Kasher suggests that Herod's war on the Nabateans was a shrewd plan to avoid supporting either Octavian or Mark Antony in the coming standoff.[14] After the Battle of Actium, in which Octavian triumphed, Herod quickly traveled to Rome, declaring that he had supported Mark Antony as duty required but was now loyal to Octavian, Caesar Augustus. Kasher contends that Herod had used the war with the Nabateans as a cover for deserting Antony sooner rather than later. Herod's short war with the Nabateans reveals his shrewd political mind, for he used that war to desert Antony while consolidating his own power and securing his borders.

After his kingship was ratified in a meeting with the victorious Octavian in Rhodes in 30 BC, Herod began to fortify his southern and eastern borders.[15] He got rid of the last of the Hasmonean claimants to his throne, accusing him of plotting a coup, and Octavian restored to Herod important towns and cities, most importantly the port of Gaza. As Kasher observes, "The military, political and economic advantages he thereby obtained were especially significant in the light of his rivalry with the Nabateans."[16]

Securing his southern and eastern frontiers and taking possession of Gaza gave Herod effective control of the all-important endpoints of the Nabatean trade routes. The Nabateans could not get their camel caravans across southern Judea without passing through Herod's checkpoints, and they could not gain access to the ships at the port of Gaza without Herod's cooperation.

Herod's forts provided military muscle for the customs posts on the trade routes through which the Nabatean caravans had to pass. These posts imposed heavy taxes on the Nabatean luxuries that were passing through. Understandably upset by Herod's tactics, the Nabateans began to support raids by bandits on his northeastern borders.

Syllaeus the Sly?

By 29 BC Herod the Great had done well. Out of the chaos of the Roman civil wars he had consolidated his power, eliminated his enemies, sealed his borders, increased his revenue stream, and become a firm favorite of the first emperor of Rome, Caesar Augustus.

For the next fifteen years Herod dealt ruthlessly with a series of rebellions, all the while keeping his eye on the Nabateans. By 14 BC the Nabateans were ready to make diplomatic overtures to Herod. The next Nabatean king, the weak and lazy Obodas III, received a loan from Herod and leased Judean land as pasture for Nabatean herds. The overtures to Herod were probably initiated by a crafty, up-and-coming Nabatean courtier named Syllaeus, who took advantage of King Obodas's weakness for his own ends.[17]

Knowing that he would need Rome's approval to become the next Nabatean king, Syllaeus formed an alliance with Herod by proposing to marry his sister Salome. Herod agreed to the match if Syllaeus would convert to Judaism. It is likely that Herod understood Syllaeus's scheme and hoped that through the marriage he would be the dominant partner when Syllaeus tried to grab the Nabatean throne.

In the meantime, Syllaeus betrayed Herod by secretly supporting the outlaws who were constantly attacking Herod's northeastern borders. When Herod struck back, Syllaeus went to Rome complaining of Herod's military action in the hope that the emperor would depose Herod. Augustus believed Syllaeus and reprimanded Herod. Pleased by Herod's demotion in the eyes of the emperor, the Nabateans continued to encourage the bandits to harass Herod's frontier.

In 9 BC King Obodas was poisoned, probably by agents of Syllaeus. Before Syllaeus could return to Petra to claim the crown, however, another courtier named Aeneas grabbed power, taking the royal name Aretas IV and offering gifts to Caesar Augustus. These gifts failed to mollify the emperor, who was enraged that Aretas would dare claim the Nabatean throne without his authority. Suddenly Herod and the new Nabatean king were on the same side: They were both enemies of Syllaeus, who was still in favor with Augustus in Rome, and they both suffered the disfavor of the emperor.

So the two kings got together. In 7 BC Herod sent a trusted confidant, Nicholas of Damascus, to Rome to make his case before Augustus. With evidence from Aretas IV and accompanied by lawyers from Aretas's court, Nicholas presented the case against Syllaeus. Convinced of Herod's correct behavior, the emperor ordered Syllaeus to pay the debts owed to Herod, and on his return to Rome in 6 BC, Augustus had Syllaeus executed.[18]

Enter Jesus of Nazareth

After a century of conflict and distrust, the new Nabatean king had teamed up with Herod's courtiers to get Herod restored to the emperor's good graces. In the same year, 6 BC, Jesus Christ was born in Bethlehem of Judea.

To see why these political maneuverings are important we should review the state of affairs at the time of Christ's birth. King Aretas IV's claim to his throne was by no means secure. He had snatched the crown from Syllaeus, who had schemed for years to depose Obodas. The emperor Augustus, still displeased with Aretas, was inclined to give the Nabatean kingdom to Herod. It was only because Herod was old and having trouble with his sons that Augustus finally received Aretas's envoys and entreaties, confirmed his rule, and punished his audacity with a mere reprimand.[19]

Despite the troubles in the past, Aretas had several strong motives to establish a good relationship with Herod, who must have felt grateful to him. First, the Nabateans and Jews were natural allies, with their shared ancestry and ancient religious ties. Herod's mother was a Nabatean princess, and he had lived as a child in the royal court of Nabatea.

Second, Herod was now in favor with Augustus—the undisputed ruler of the Roman Empire—and an alliance with Herod would help Aretas shore up the emperor's shaky support.

Third, Herod was old and dying, and the succession to his throne was uncertain. If a prince was born to the Herodian dynasty, the new king of the Nabateans would do well to be the first to pay homage.

Finally, Herod had fortified his border with Nabatea, and Augustus had given him the port of Gaza. To get their goods to Rome, the Nabateans needed to cross that border, pass through Herod's customs posts, and travel across his territory to Gaza. With Augustus's accession as emperor, peace was on the horizon. It was an opportune time to build bridges, not walls.

Marriage between royal houses has always been a way to cement alliances and build trust. We know that Aretas IV and Herod were forging an alliance at the time of Christ's birth because soon after Herod's death two years later, his heir, Herod Antipas, married Aretas IV's daughter Phasaelis.[20]

Political realities were therefore driving Aretas IV to make overtures to Herod. At the same time political realities were driving Herod and the Parthians apart. In 37 BC the Parthians had been forcefully expelled from Judea by the Romans. The Parthian king, Phraates IV, was bound by a treaty with Caesar Augustus to remain east of the Euphrates River. Were the Magi from Persia-Parthia? Phraates had no motivation to risk a breach with Rome by sending a diplomatic entourage to King Herod's court. Neither did the barbaric and venal Phraates IV have any religious motivation to send magi to Jerusalem.

Aretas IV of Nabatea, on the other hand, had every motivation to send envoys to Herod's court. We have examined the Nabateans' ancient links with both the Jewish and Babylonian-Persian cultures and have seen that the magi were dispersed across the ancient Middle East, but especially in Arabia. We have deduced that, because of their culture, history, and religion, Nabatean wise men would have a natural interest in a Jewish Messiah.

If Nabatean stargazers discerned that a new king of the Jews was to be born, the political circumstances meshed perfectly for a high-level visit. What better way to consolidate a good relationship with Augustus than for Aretas IV to send his own magian diplomats to Herod's court with rich, royal gifts of tribute?

The gifts of gold, frankincense, and myrrh were more than simply luxurious gifts for a king, however. These three treasures provide further evidence of the true identity of the wise men.

CHAPTER NINE

The Three Treasures

Giving and receiving gifts is part of the delight of Christmas, and the tradition that the Christ child himself received rich gifts of gold, frankincense and myrrh provide an extra sparkle of charm to what is already a wonderful custom. Meanwhile, as the Christian story of the wise men was passed down, the three gifts also assumed profound religious symbolism.

Gold stood for the kingly status of the infant and his mother. Frankincense was used in worship and so marks the Christ child as a prophet and priest. Myrrh was used for embalming the dead, so it pointed to the boy's ultimate, tragic, redemptive death.[1]

The problem is that the religious symbolism is all part of the later, fanciful accretions to the story. Matthew says nothing about the symbolism of the gifts, simply reporting, "They opened their treasures and presented to him gold, frankincense and myrrh" (Matthew 2:11). As the legends developed around the Magi story, the three gifts also became the foundation for the idea that there were three wise men. Furthermore, the implied reference to royalty in Psalm 72:10–11[2] and Isaiah 60:11[3] inspired early Christians to conclude not only that there were three wise men but also that they were kings. While such conclusions are understandable, Matthew's text does not number the wise men at three, nor does he identify them as kings.

As the legends developed, Christian writers pondered the religious symbolism of the gifts, but very few have paid closer attention to the significance of the gifts themselves. Commentators have simply considered them to be appropriately luxurious gift items. Knowing about the Nabatean incense trade, and assuming that the Magi were from Persia, some writers have suggested that the Persian Magi stopped by Petra on their way to Bethlehem to buy the gifts.[4]

The gifts of gold, frankincense, and myrrh are indeed deeply significant, not because of their mystical religious meaning, and not because they imply that the wise men were three kings. They are important to the story because they point unmistakably to the Nabatean magi at the court of Aretas IV as the true identity of the wise men.

Gold from the Queen of Sheba

The legends that grew up around the Magi invariably link the wise men to the Queen of Sheba's visit to Solomon in the tenth century BC. After all, the first Jewish Christians believed Jesus was the long-awaited heir of David and Solomon. As the Queen of Sheba came from the East with rich gifts to the court of Solomon (1 Kings 10:1–13), so the "three kings" travelled from distant eastern lands to the court of the newborn king—the son of David and successor of Solomon.

Some see the link and wonder whether Matthew's story about the Magi was therefore intentionally crafted as a prophecy fulfillment.[5] After all, Matthew records Jesus' own comments regarding the Queen of Sheba visiting Solomon, saying about himself, "one greater than Solomon is here" (Matthew 12:42). The Bible scholars also suspect Matthew of devising the story as a fulfillment of Isaiah 60 and Psalm 72.[6]

In these two Old Testament passages the psalmist and the prophet are looking forward to a day when the glory of Israel will be restored and the surrounding kingdoms will come to give tribute. So Isaiah writes, "Herds of camels will cover your land, young camels of Midian and Ephah. And all from Sheba will come, bearing gold and incense and proclaiming the praise of the Lord."

Was Matthew creating a story about the infant Christ in order to make it seem as if his birth fulfilled Old Testament prophecies? It is possible, but the problem with this theory is that Matthew is usually explicit when he sees a fulfillment of prophecy. He prefaces a story about Jesus with, "so it might be fulfilled as the prophet has written." He doesn't do this with the Magi story.

Furthermore, if the Magi story was fashioned out of whole cloth to make Jesus' birth more special and fulfill prophecies, Matthew didn't do a very good job of it. The Queen of Sheba came to Solomon, but the wise men came first to Herod the Great. The paranoid murderer Herod was hardly an apt parallel to the wise and good King Solomon. Furthermore, if Matthew were crafting a story that fulfilled the prophecy of Isaiah, to make it match he should have mentioned camels, and he should *not* have included myrrh.

The fact is, we don't need to theorize that the Magi story was invented long after Matthew's original gospel to make Jesus seem more special. The bare-bones account in Matthew fits the facts as we know them. The three gifts are not legendary, luxurious gifts presented by exotic, foreign kings, nor are they mystical symbols of the Christ child's identity and destiny.

Instead they are the ordinary currencies and commodities of the Middle East in the first century. When we examine the use and provenance of the three gifts we find they help to root the story not in legend and religious symbolism, but in cultural, political, and economic realities.

The International Gold Standard

As it is today, so it was from time immemorial: Gold is an international currency. It is not only used to buy goods, and it is not only the most beautiful and luxurious metal. Gold is the mark of true security, wealth, and power. It is the gift and possession of monarchs and millionaires.

Gold was also one of the sources of the fabulous wealth of the Nabateans. Gold is still mined in Saudi Arabia today.[7] In ancient times Arabian gold was considered the finest in the world, thought to be "so pure that no smelting was necessary."[8] It was also mined during the early Islamic period, and throughout the Old Testament we find records of the famed gold mines of Arabia.[9]

In the Nabatean region of northwest Arabia (also called "Hejaz") is the ancient, incredibly wealthy gold mine called the *Mahd adh Dhahab* or "Cradle of Gold." Archaeologists Juris Zarins of Missouri State University and Farouk El-Baz of Boston University suggest that the Pishon River from the legendary gold-rich land of Havilah[10] may be the now dried up riverbed that once flowed northeast from the area around three thousand years ago.

In the mid-nineteenth century, the British explorer Richard Burton first discovered the gold mines in the area, calling them the Gold Mines of Midian.[11] Others have identified the site as the legendary King Solomon's gold mine.[12] Whatever the speculation, archaeologists have discovered at the site "huge quantities of waste rock...left by the ancient miners, still containing traces of gold. Thousands of stone hammers and grindstones used to extract the gold from the ore litter the mine slopes."[13]

In addition to the ancient Cradle of Gold in northwestern Arabia, the southern kingdom of Saba (in modern day Yemen) was also famous for its gold mines in its East African territories. In 2012 a team of British archaeologists uncovered the remains of a vast Sabean gold mine in Ethiopia.[14] The mines dated from the eighth century BC when the Sabean kingdom was flourishing.[15]

While gold mining existed in Arabia for centuries, by the end of the first millennium BC the center of international trade shifted north.[16] And by the time of King Aretas IV, the Nabateans had long controlled not only northern Arabia but also the vital routes from gold-rich Saba. The Nabateans' series of fortified ports and strictly controlled trade routes meant they monitored the flow of gold from Saba and the mines of East Africa. Consequently, gold was not simply a luxurious gift item to be brought to a newborn king of the Jews, it was also one of the "cash crops" of the Nabatean kingdom of Aretas IV.

Frankincense and Myrrh

The value of gold is timeless, but the precious quality of the wise men's other two gifts is not immediately obvious to people of the twenty-first century. To understand the immense value of frankincense, one needs to grasp the universal practice of religion in the ancient world.

Most people not only believed in the supernatural realm, they also practiced religion. Part of their religious duty was to burn incense in the temples of their gods and goddesses. They believed the gods were "up there" in the spiritual realm, and the theory was that the gods were pleased with the fragrant smoke that ascended from the earthly altars as prayers.[17]

The Jews were no exception. Their portable tabernacle, which was eventually replaced by the temple in Jerusalem, featured a golden altar where a specially prescribed mixture of incense was offered morning and night with enough incense to burn continually.[18]

The Jews had probably learned about the use of incense from the Egyptians. The first mention of the use of incense in worship is in Egyptian texts from the third millennium BC. Its use spread to Mesopotamia, and by Roman times, in pagan temples across the empire, incense was offered to the gods daily.[19] "The growth of Rome had ushered in a period of almost obsessive incense burning. Besides its uses in medicine and worship, no Roman funeral was complete without vast quantities of frankincense whose fragrant smoke was thought put in a good word to the gods for the welfare of the departed."[20]

Like frankincense, myrrh was made from a gum resin, dried and compressed and burnt to produce an aromatic smoke. In addition to the fragrant smoke it was also used as a rich perfume. "Myrrh, an analgesic, was also used to treat conditions ranging from battle wound to skin inflammations. The Greek physician Hippocrates prescribed it for sores and the Romans used it to treat worm infestation, coughs and certain infections."[21] Jesus was offered wine mingled with myrrh as a pain killer at the crucifixion (Matthew 27:34).

The frankincense was tapped from trees that only grew in southern Arabia and limited areas of East Africa.[22] The myrrh came from a wider area in southern Arabia.[23] But both frankincense and myrrh could only be harvested once a year. The production was labor intensive and the yield small. Nevertheless, the quantities of frankincense and myrrh the Arabians produced were huge.

The fifth-century-BC, Greek historian Herodotus reported that the Arabians sent an annual tribute of one thousand talents (over twenty-seven tons) of incense to Darius of Persia.[24] When Alexander the Great conquered the port city of Gaza he found huge reserves of frankincense and myrrh in the storehouses and sent a gift of five hundred talents (13.7 tons) of frankincense and one hundred talents of myrrh to an old tutor who had once told him not to waste such precious gifts.[25]

The value of the frankincense and myrrh was determined then as the value of commodities is determined now: supply and demand. The demand was high and the supply was low. Therefore frankincense and myrrh were some of the most valuable commodities in the ancient Middle East.

Nabatean expert Jane Taylor tracked down an account from the historian Pliny about the specific amount of money a Nabatean trader could be expected to make. Once taxes and duties were paid there was a profit of nearly $1,000 for each heavily laden camel. Considering there were many hundreds of camels in a caravan, one trip could yield a profit of up to $100,000 for a team of traders to share.[26]

Gifts of Tribute

Gold, frankincense, and myrrh were, without a doubt, the richest of gifts that could be offered to a newborn king. But their significance lies not so much in their religious symbolism or in the fabulous wealth they represented. Instead the gifts themselves are clues to the identity of the wise men.

Throughout the ancient Middle East, gifts were given and received as diplomatic gestures. Josephus records how, when Herod completed building the city of Caesarea Maritima in 9 BC, envoys from many nations came to Palestine with gifts.[27] The gifts would not simply be luxurious, they would also represent the finest produce from the country of origin.

Likewise, when a military leader conquered a country, the neighboring rulers would approach him to offer gifts of tribute, hoping that he would not invade their territory and impose heavy taxes. "Countless Eastern potentates...returning from mission, brought home 'gifts' from grateful allies: exotic animals...wagons full of food, and the golden wreaths."[28] Pierre Briant records the gifts made to the Persian King Darius after his successful invasion of North Africa: "The Colchians and Ethiopians sent a hundred boys and a hundred girls as slaves. The Ethiopians brought 'two quarts of unrefined gold, two hundred logs of ebony, and twenty elephant tusks.' The Arabians brought a thousand talents of frankincense."[29] If tribute was not offered it was often demanded by a conquering monarch.

Thus, after rebellions in Arabia were crushed by the Assyrians, the rulers of seven Arabian tribes were forced to make tribute gifts of gold, silver, male and female camels, and "all kinds of spices."[30] The tribute gifts of Arabians in particular were gold, frankincense, and myrrh. So in the eighth century BC, the scribes of the Assyrian king Tiglath-Pileser III recorded that he was sent gifts of tribute from the Sabeans of southern Arabia of the riches of their land, which were gold and camels and frankincense and myrrh.[31]

"The three treasures that the magi presented to Christ formed a primary source for the economic power and wealth of the territory of Arabia over a very lengthy period of time."[32] The Nabateans traded goods from India, China, East Africa, and beyond, but gold, frankincense, and myrrh were their own unique products. The Magi therefore gave what must be understood as diplomatic gifts representative of their own country.[33]

When the psalmist writes, "Kings of Tarshish and the isles shall bring him tribute, The kings of Saba shall offer gifts,"[34] the Jews would have understood these royal treasures as offerings acknowledging their allegiance to the king. Furthermore, not only were tribute gifts given to conquering kings, it was also customary for neighboring monarchs to offer gifts at the birth of a future king.[35]

In 6 BC the political situation between the Nabatean King Aretas IV and Herod the Great was exactly what you would expect for tribute gifts to be made. Aretas's claim to the throne was shaky. Herod had just worked with the lawyers in Aretas's court to persuade the emperor Augustus that their joint enemy Syllaeus was a scoundrel. Aretas had already sent tribute gifts to Caesar, who grudgingly accepted the gifts and gave his approval to Aretas IV's claims.[36] If Aretas sent sweeteners to Caesar it makes sense that he would do the same for Herod when the proper opportunity arose.

Furthermore, Augustus had returned the crucial port of Gaza to Herod, so it was vital for Aretas IV to remain in Herod's good graces. When the wise men of his court announced that they had discerned from the stars that a new king of the Jews was to be born, Aretas IV would have had every motive to send envoys to Herod's court in Jerusalem to present gifts that were not only rich and regal but also representative of the wealth and power of Aretas's Nabatean kingdom. Therefore, while the wise men were not kings themselves, as courtiers they did represent King Aretas IV.

The Incense Trail

Gold, frankincense, and myrrh point to the identity of the wise men not only because they were representative tribute gifts of the Arabian kingdom but also because the Nabatean trade routes ran directly past Jerusalem and Bethlehem.

The Incense Route was an ancient series of trails used by the camel caravans that criss-crossed the desert. The Nabateans' capital of Petra stood halfway between the opening to the Gulf of Aqaba and the Dead Sea at a point where the North-South trade route from Arabia to Damascus was crossed by the East-West route from Yemen to Gaza. This position gave the Nabateans a hold over the trade in both directions.

Caravans coming from the North, East, and South would meet in Petra to make their way west to Gaza. The road to Gaza ran past a series of forts. The ruins of the four Nabatean towns of Haluza, Mamshit, Avdat, and Shivta, with their associated fortresses, can still be visited today. Located in southern Israel, they are staging posts linking Petra to the Mediterranean. Following this trade route, the Nabatean Magi would have passed just ninety miles south of Jerusalem.

The road north to Damascus would take them past Bethlehem to Jerusalem. The Nabatean Magi would have known the area well. They did not need a star to guide them to the palace of Herod the Great. Furthermore, after their visit to Bethlehem, knowing the secret paths of the Arabian desert, they could easily have eluded Herod and, as Matthew writes, "gone home to their country by another route."

Matthew doesn't mention it, but the wise men would have had another reason to return to their own territory by a different route. Herod would have known they were Nabatean magi from the court of Aretas IV. At that time the two kings were forging a fresh alliance. If the wise men had incurred Herod's wrath, no doubt Herod would have alerted Aretas to their existence. Would not Aretas also have been on the lookout for his diplomats who had infuriated his ally Herod? It would make sense to conclude that instead of going south and east back to Petra the Magi reversed their direction and took the road north to Damascus.

Camels and Long Journeys?

That the Nabateans were neighbors to Judea and their trade caravans passed regularly through Herod's territories reveals two other misconceptions about the Magi story. The legends that have come down to us invariably speak of the Magi making a long and arduous journey through unfamiliar terrain. But nowhere in Matthew's account is there any mention of a long-distance trek, nor does he say they travelled through foreign territory. All that was read into the story later.

Matthew simply says, "Wise men came from the East."

We will see in chapter eleven why this short phrase is so revealing. For now, suffice it to say that the wise men did not come a long distance from Persia, India, Africa or China. They did not travel through unknown territory guided by a miraculous star. They came a comparatively short way to a destination familiar to them on roads that were well known.

Did they come on camels? Matthew does not mention camels.

Certainly, the tribes of Arabia were famous for domesticating camels and using them in their trade caravans. They gave camels to Assyrian kings as tribute gifts and bred camels for sale and trade. However, during the reign of King Aretas III the Nabateans adopted more Greek ways, and one of the results was the increased use of the horse as an honorable means of transport. "Camels continued to be pack animals, but horses were desired by those wishing to ride in style. The famous Nabatean camel cavalry was soon replaced by horse riding Nabateans."[37]

With their usual entrepreneurial ingenuity, the Nabateans not only began to use horses, they also bred horses that were uniquely excellent. Arabian horses are still a famous breed today. Known for their light-footedness and swift speed, they were also prized for their endurance, intelligence, and gentleness. The contemporary of Herod the Great, Nabatean King Malichus I, gave Julius Caesar two thousand horses for his military campaign in Egypt, while Josephus records that King Malichus II sent Emperor Titus one thousand cavalry to help in his attack on Jerusalem in AD 70.

Were the Magi exotic kings from Persia and India? Did they make a long trek across a hostile and unfamiliar desert on camels? Traditionalists will be disappointed to learn that the wise men were Nabatean courtiers on horseback traveling a few hundred miles to Jerusalem on their own well-travelled trade routes.

Worship and Homage

Most Christians in the West are influenced by the noble words of the King James version of the Bible, which translates verse eleven of Matthew's Magi story as saying that the wise men "fell down and worshipped him."

Most other English versions echo this translation, saying the wise men "bowed down and worshipped him" or "knelt and worshipped." We use the word "worship" in a religious context, and the prevailing myth about the wise men is that they were mystics or religious seekers. The elaborated story is that the spiritual wise men set out on a mystical quest to find the incarnate Son of God and, finding him, offered their hearts and lives in religious worship.

However, this interpretation is too easy. It shows a later religious bias and a lack of understanding of Matthew's time, place, and context.

When King Tiridates made his journey to give tribute to Nero in AD 66 he said, "I have come to you my god, to pay homage, as I do to Mithras."[38] This event shows how the political and religious elements of kingship were understood in the ancient world. The gifts of tribute were not merely a diplomatic nicety, a down payment on taxes or a political bribe. They were also a religious offering.

In the ancient world the king was, at least, God's appointee, and at most he was considered to be a god or a son of God. The gifts of tribute were linked with an act of submission that not only acknowledged the superior wealth and power of the monarch but also his divinity.

The traditional translation that the wise men "worshipped" Jesus is therefore misleading. Other translations rightly translate, "they prostrated themselves and did him homage."[39] However, the fact that the wise men were employed on a diplomatic mission does not exclude a religious dimension. The wise men were, after all, spiritual as well as political advisors. The astral and prophetic aspect of Nabatean religion means the wise men from Petra may very well have understood their homage to have a religious dimension as well as a diplomatic motivation. In paying homage to a newborn king they were also giving tribute to a divine being.

Searching for a Savior

We have seen in the last chapter how, throughout the ancient world, there was an expectation of a world leader who would bring justice and peace. That leader was expected to arise from among the Jews. Influenced by the Abrahamic Judaism of Arabia, the Nabatean Magi would almost certainly have known of the Old Testament messianic prophecies—especially those of Isaiah.

Therefore, their diplomatic mission from the court of Aretas IV to Herod the Great would have held for them a deeper mystery and expectation. If the prophecies were to be believed, a great king would arise from among the Jews. But how did they know the prophecy was about to come true?

The one aspect of the story we have not yet examined is the mysterious star. The history, culture, location, politics, and religion of the Nabateans all point to their identity as the wise men of Bethlehem, but it was the appearance of the "Star of Bethlehem" that prompted them to embark on their mission.

CHAPTER TEN

The Star of Bethlehem

In the popular Christmas story, the Star of Bethlehem is a miraculous celestial sign that moved through the night sky, guiding the wise men on an arduous journey through harsh desert lands to the humble birthplace of Jesus Christ. Christmas cards and Nativity plays perpetuate the myth of the magical star, but astronomers point out that stars are fixed points. They don't move across the sky from one place to another.

Of course, it's not quite as simple as that. While stars are indeed fixed points, they appear to move because of the Earth's rotation. Their apparent movement and the complexity of various astral phenomena make the Star of Bethlehem the most intriguing aspect of the Magi story. Astronomers, astrologers, and amateur researchers have come up with a bewildering array of theories about the star the wise men reported.

A Supernatural Miracle Star?

Bradley Schaefer, a physicist and astronomer, writes, "All of the attempted explanations [of the Star of Bethlehem] can be categorized as one of the following: a pious fable, an astronomical event, a miracle, or an astrological horoscope."[1]

Let's first consider the first and third of these possible explanations. If the star was simply a feature of a pious fairy tale, we wouldn't be this far along in this book for we would have concluded that there was not a historical star and moved on. Might the star have been a divine celestial portent—a miracle worked by God himself?

The idea that the star was a supernatural phenomenon that moved across the night sky began with the gnostic myths that were concocted about the Magi. In the Syrian Infancy Gospel, the star is an angel who leads the wise men to Jesus. In the ludicrously fanciful "Legend of Aphroditianus," a star appears in a pagan temple in which the statues have come alive and are dancing. The star then leads the Magi across the desert on their mystical quest. In *The Revelation of the Magi*, the star appears as a blazing baby in the sky who tells the wise men to go on the journey. It floats before them in the night sky, performing miracles along the way.

These ridiculous gnostic myths contributed to the assumption that the star was a celestial magic show, an assumption that evolved into legend. Because most believers down the ages have taken for granted the miraculous nature of the star, critical scholars have dismissed the whole Magi story as a pious fiction.

When You Wish upon a Star

How did Matthew understand the star sign? It is possible that he believed it was a miraculous intervention by God. Furthermore, we should not rule out a supernatural solution. It could be that God produced a miraculous star that moved across the night sky and led the wise men to the Christ child. But questions arise.

If a supernaturally mobile star guided the wise men, why didn't it take them directly to Bethlehem instead of leading them first to Jerusalem? If the star was a visible supernatural intervention, why didn't everyone see it moving across the night sky? Indeed, why isn't such a stupendous phenomenon recorded in the annals of ancient stargazers? We have astronomical records from ancient Greece, Babylon, and China. Why no mention of the amazing moving star from around 6 BC?

If the star was of supernatural origin, perhaps it was like those apparitions to mystics which only certain persons "see"—the sun spinning at Fatima or the Virgin Mary appearing to chosen visionaries. Matthew's account doesn't sound like that, however. It is more matter-of-fact. Nevertheless, while we should not rule out the possibility of a miracle or vision, we should rely on common sense. We are right to be skeptical of supernatural solutions.

Matthew, of course, never says that a supernatural star guided the wise men across the desert. He mentions the star twice. First the wise men say to Herod, "Where is the one who has been born king of the Jews? We saw his star when it rose and have come to worship him" (Matthew 2:2). A few verses later Matthew continues, "After they had heard the king, they went on their way, and the star they had seen when it rose went ahead of them until it stopped over the place where the child was" (Matthew 2:9).

Because the gnostic infancy narratives became part of the tradition, everyone assumes that the star led the Magi throughout their journey, but that is not what the gospel actually says. Matthew says the wise men saw the star "when it rose" before their journey and then a second time after meeting with Herod when it directed them to Bethlehem, where it stopped. The Christmas traditions say the star guided them on a long journey, but as we will see, there are other explanations that make better sense and are more faithful to

Matthew's text. We should rely on a supernatural explanation only when we have ruled out all the natural possibilities. Therefore, if it was not a supernatural event, could the Star of Bethlehem have been a natural, observable, celestial phenomenon?

A Natural Astronomical Event?

This is where the astronomers become interested and excited, and this is where the scriptwriters for Christmas planetarium shows come into their own. The theory is that a comet, supernova, meteor, or conjunction of planets produced a spectacular display that convinced the wise men to go on a search for the infant king of the Jews.

Using sophisticated computer technology that reproduces the night sky at any place and on any date in history, astronomers have pored over the charts to find suitably spectacular stellar events. Bradley Schaefer has identified more than a dozen such events in the decade of Christ's birth. The problem with this explanation of the Star of Bethlehem, he explains, is that "all decades are crowded with spectacular astronomical events."[2] This has not stopped astronomers from proposing their theories.

One of the most famous proposals is that the star was Halley's Comet. The seventeenth-century astronomer Johannes Kepler proposed that the star was a triple conjunction that spawned a supernova,[3] while in our own day the astronomer Sir Patrick Moore has theorized that it was two separate meteors.[4] Richard Coates and David Sergeant think it was an ordinary fixed star that took on special astrological significance.[5] Colin Nicholl and Colin Humphreys argue that the Star of Bethlehem was a comet.[6]

Each of these astronomical theories, however, invites commonsense objections. To begin with, if there are so many "spectacular astronomical events," are they really so spectacular? While the various stars, novas, supernovas, comets, and planetary conjunctions might have been impressive, were they really so unusual? If the astral event identified with the Star of Bethlehem was so spectacular, why didn't everyone see it, and why didn't the ancient astronomers record it? Some theoreticians point out that Chinese astronomers did record a spectacular comet in 5 BC, but shouldn't such a comet also have been seen and recorded by Roman or Mesopotamian stargazers?

More problematically, why would stargazers in ancient Persia or India, seeing a meteor, supernova, or comet, take it as a sign that a new king was to be born hundreds of miles away in Judea? And why would they regard such news as so religiously significant that they should embark on a long, expensive, and dangerous journey in search of a Jewish Son of God?

An unusual stellar display does not, on its own, explain the journey to Jerusalem. If there was a spectacular astral event, something else must have motivated the observers to connect that event with the birth of Jewish royalty.

With three of the four solutions seeming improbable, we are left with the astrological explanation. According to this theory, the "star" was not a spectacular astronomical display but an alignment of the planets that astrologers interpreted as a sign that a child who would rule over the Jewish people was about to be born.

Ancient Astrology

In our age the idea that the stars determine our identity and our destiny is dismissed as so much silly superstition. It was not so in ancient times.

We make clear distinctions between astronomy, astrology, and religion, but as Courtney Roberts, a historian of astrology, explains, "this was not always the case. These three—science, religion, and astrology—were intricately intertwined throughout much of human history. Francesca Rochberg makes the same point...: 'Celestial divination, astronomical observation, and astrological computation represent interdependent parts of a multifaceted and complex tradition of celestial science in ancient Mesopotamia.'"[7]

Roberts chronicles the rise of astrology in the ancient world. In ancient Mesopotamia, early astrologers took the first step from simple animistic religion—the belief that natural bodies like planets and stars are manifestations of gods and goddesses—concluding that if the stars and planets were gods and goddesses, then they must have personalities and behave in a rational and predictable manner.

Believing that what occurred above was reflected in the world below, soothsayers tried to predict earthly events by studying the behavior of the stars. Jewish tradition suggests that Abraham—who originated in Mesopotamia and may have worshipped the moon god Sin—was also adept in astrological lore.[8] The earliest attempts at astrology were simple predictions and omens, often combining the study of the stars with other crude forms of augury like ornithomancy (foretelling the future by observing bird flight and song), haruspicy (animal entrails), and oneiromancy (dreams).

Around the seventh and eighth centuries BC, the astrologers of Mesopotamia began to take a more structured and analytical approach to their astrology. They moved from producing crude omens to deducing more specific predictions. In the seventh century they began to develop zodiacs to systematize their predictions.

In the centuries that followed, there was a growing awareness that a person was born under a particular star sign. And by the time of the birth of Christ, astrology had evolved from mere fatalism into a philosophy that embraced personal interaction with one's destiny. The Magi astrologers who visited the Christ child would have believed that if one could understand the pattern of the movements in the heavens, one could not only predict what might happen on Earth but also engage one's will and actively cooperate with destiny.

The ancient astrologers' primary tool was the zodiac, a chart of the constellations used to analyze the movements of the planets and deduce their significance. With the zodiac, an astrologer can draw up a horoscope, a chart of the locations of the sun, moon, and planets at a particular point in time. A natal horoscope, based on the date of a child's birth, supposedly explains the personality and destiny of the child. By charting the regular movement of the planets, the astrologer believes, it is also possible to predict what might happen in the future.

The astrological explanation for the Star of Bethlehem solves two recurring problems. First, it answers the difficulty of the star's not being seen by most people. According to the astrological theory, the "star" was not an astral display that anyone could observe by looking up into the sky. Instead, it was an unusual configuration of planets and constellations—the significance of which would have been observed and understood only by those adept in astrology.

Second, the whole point of astrology is to read the movements of the planets and predict events on Earth. There would have been no motivation for someone who simply observed an unusual astral display to journey to Bethlehem. However, an astrologer, who was constantly reading the constellations, might have discerned in the stars tidings of a Jewish king and, given his circumstances, might have been highly motivated to set out to find that prince and pay him homage.

The history of astrology supports the veracity of the Magi story. What we read in Matthew's account aligns perfectly with what is known about the astrological theories of the time. In his study of the history of Mesopotamian astrology and its migration into Greek thought and Jewish culture, Edwin Yamauchi writes, "I would conclude that we can best understand the story of the Magi in Matthew not as a literary creation, but as a historical episode."[9]

The Astrological Answer

The first thing to grasp about the astrological theory is that the "star" was not what we understand as a star. It was a planet. The language of the Bible does not distinguish stars from planets as we do. Therefore when Matthew quotes the wise men—"We have seen his star rising"—the astrological theory maintains that they were referring to a planet, not a star.

Probably the most popular astrological explanation is that there was a triple conjunction of the planets Jupiter and Saturn in 7 BC.

David Hughes and Simo Parpola contend that these two planets came together three times in one year, an extremely rare event that the astrologers in Babylon understood to indicate the birth of a powerful king.[10]

In his 1999 book, *The Star of Bethlehem: The Legacy of the Magi*,[11] the astronomer Michael Molnar argues along similar lines. He had been studying ancient astrological texts for years before he deduced that the Star of Bethlehem was actually an astrological—rather than a simple astronomical—phenomenon.

The study of astrology is extremely arcane, demanding a thorough knowledge of astronomy as well as astrological theory. Understanding the intricacies of ancient astrology demands even more expertise. Molnar, one of the experts, lays out an interesting case that the Magi observed certain signs in the heavens that convinced them of the imminent birth of a king of the Jews, and I will summarize his argument.

Ancient astrologers associated a country with a particular constellation. So, for example, Babylon might be associated with Taurus, Italy with Leo, and Persia with Virgo. Although theories vary, Molnar believes astrologers at the time of Christ associated Judea with the constellation Aries. The planet Jupiter and the moon, moreover, were associated with royalty. On ancient coins and in carvings, for example, a blazing star (the sign for a planet) and a crescent moon indicate royalty.[12]

With these associations in mind, Molnar searched the astronomical record for an unusual conjunction of the moon and Jupiter in the constellation Aries near the time of Jesus' birth. He found one on April 17, 6 BC. Jupiter was rising in the constellation Aries, but with a "lunar occultation." In other words, the planet was hidden by, or very close to, the moon. Astrologers believed that the presence of the moon strengthened the royal significance of Jupiter.

At the same time, Jupiter was at its "heliacal rising"—it was appearing on the horizon at the same time as, or just before, the sun. On April 17, 6 BC, the royal planet Jupiter was rising with the sun and was embraced by the moon, a highly unusual phenomenon and, according to astrological theory, an indication of an amazingly powerful royal presence. This conjunction of Jupiter and the moon in the constellation Aries revealed to the astrologers that a great king would be born in Judea.

Molnar believes two of the phrases in Matthew's account actually indicate knowledge of these astrological principles. The New International Version of the Bible translates Matthew 2:2 as, "Where is the one who has been born king of the Jews? We saw his star when it rose and have come to worship him." Remembering that "star" just as easily means "planet," Molnar theorizes that the phrase "We saw his star when it rose" means that the wise men witnessed the all-important heliacal rising of Jupiter on April 17, 6 BC.

Molnar's theory also explains the curious detail in Matthew's account that the star they had seen "went before them and stopped where the child was." Astronomers point out that planets on the move don't "stop" over anything. Molnar, however, believes that Mathew's description refers to a "planetary retrograde motion and stationing."[13] "As the Earth moves in its orbit, it speeds past Jupiter and produces the illusion that Jupiter halts and reverses its motion against the background stars."[14]

The Magi were already on their way to Bethlehem, having been sent there by Herod. As they traveled the few miles south, Jupiter appeared to reverse its progress across the sky and stop just as they reached Bethlehem. According to Ptolemy—one of the most important astrologers of antiquity—a retrograde motion and stationing strengthens the celestial effects on earthly events.[15] Knowing this, the Magi were, as Matthew records, overjoyed.

Starry, Starry Night

The problem with Molnar's theory is that the heliacal rising would not have been visible to the wise men. They could have predicted it, but Matthew reports that they "saw his star." If you begin studying the Star of Bethlehem, it will not be long before you discover that there are as many theories about the star as there are stars in the heavens. Ernest L. Martin also believes the Star of Bethlehem can be traced back to the astrological conjunction of various planets.[16] He tracks various occultations of Jupiter in 7 BC and reads into them the suitable astrological interpretations.

Rick Larson, an amateur Biblical scholar, thinks he has found an astrological solution to the mysterious Star of Bethlehem. In his documentary film *The Star of Bethlehem*, he suggests that a conjunction of Venus and Jupiter in the constellation Leo in 3–2 BC is the "star" the wise men saw. Jupiter's moving around the "king star" Regulus is also thought to be significant. Like Molnar, Larson suggests that Matthew's description of the star's moving to Bethlehem and stopping over the house of the Christ child can be attributed to the "retrograde and stopping" appearance of a planet.

The physicist and astronomer Aaron Adair has problems with Larson's theory.[17] He points out that the celestial phenomena on which it depends are from 3–2 BC. Jesus, however, was born during the reign of Herod the Great, who died in 4 BC. Furthermore, there is no historical evidence for Larson's assumption that the constellation Leo was associated with the Jews. Ancient astrologers did attribute geographical and national significance to certain star signs, but none of them connected Leo with Judea or the Jews.

The Great Christ Comet

Martin's and Larson's theories have been challenged, and Molnar's theory also has its scholarly critics.[18] The Biblical scholar Colin Nicholl, for his part, has done a masterly job of poking holes in all the different theories while proposing his own intricately argued hypothesis that the Star of Bethlehem was an amazing comet.

In his astonishing book *The Great Christ Comet*, Nicholl contends that the Star of Bethlehem was a visible astral phenomenon that also had great astrological significance: a "narrowly inclined, retrograde, long period comet."[19] He assumes, like most people, that the Magi were from Babylon, but the charts of the night sky he relies on are as applicable to the Nabatean territory as to Babylon. Nicholl's theory is unique in connecting the signs the Magi would have seen to visionary accounts in the book of Revelation, pagan religions of the ancient Middle East, and Old Testament prophecies. Like the other theories, Nicholl's has flaws—not least of which is the lack of any astronomical record of such a comet in the Middle East at the time.[20]

Nicholl is on the same track as the archaeoastronomer Mark Kidger and Cambridge scientist Colin Humphreys, each of whom offers a version of what is probably the best solution. They posit that the wise men were influenced by several different celestial events around 6 BC.[21] Humphreys summarizes:

> It is suggested that a combination of three unusual and significant astronomical events caused the Magi to set off on their journey. First there was a triple conjunction of Saturn and Jupiter in the constellation Pisces in 7 b.c. Such an event occurs only every 900 years.... Second, in 6 b.c. there was a massing of the three planets Mars, Saturn and Jupiter in Pisces. Such a massing only occurs every 800 years (and very much more infrequently in Pisces).... Third, a comet appeared in 5 b.c. in the east in the constellation Capricornus. In the astrology of the times a comet in the east signified a rapidly approaching event.[22]

While none of these theories is absolutely watertight, Nicholl, Molnar, Humphreys, and the other researchers make a convincing case that the Star of Bethlehem was not a pious fable or a supernatural event. Instead the star was a genuine astronomical phenomenon that was loaded with astrological significance.

Astrology and Prophecy

Were the Jews interested in astrology? The Old Testament condemns astrology (Leviticus 19:26; Deuteronomy 18:9–12) and regards
it as useless.[23] Some, however, propose that Father Abraham's religion
was rooted in the Babylonian worship of the moon god.[24] While
astrology was questionable for the Jews, it was not unheard of.

Certainly, during the time of the Babylonian exile, when the
Nabatean civilization was forming, Judaism was influenced by the
wisdom and philosophy of the astrologers.[25] The scholars J. C. Green-
field and M. Sokoloff have presented "an astonishing variety of texts
revealing the Jewish fascination with Mesopotamian stellar religion,
lunar omens, astrological physiognomy, and natal and predictive
astrology."[26] Yamauchi has also shown the importance of Mesopotamian astrology for the Jews.[27]

Yamauchi explains that the astrology of the Babylonian magi was
diffused across the ancient world.[28] This blend of Babylonian and
Jewish influences was acknowledged by the eleventh-century Iranian
scholar Al-Biriuni, who wrote that the religion of the neighboring
Sabaean culture of southern Arabia involved "star worship" and was
a "'system mixed up of Magism and Judaism.'"[29] If that was true of
the Sabaean culture, it is a fair conclusion, given the historical evidence, that the Nabatean religion was also a blend of Judaism and
magian astral religion.

At the time of Christ's birth, on the borders of the Nabatean
kingdom was the Essene community at Qumran, for whom astrology
was important, as we saw in chapter seven. We know that the religion
of the Essenes at Qumran also had a strong apocalyptic and messianic
dimension. The Dead Sea Scrolls, among other texts, reveal that the
prophecies of Isaiah were vitally important to them.

Taking all the evidence together we can recognize that different forms
of prophecy—including astrology—were vital to the religions of the
ancient Middle East. The wise men, therefore, would have been strongly
influenced by the prophetic texts that pointed to a coming Messiah.

This is where Colin Nicholl's study becomes most fascinating. He shows how the astrological signs of his proposed comet connect with the ancient myths and the messianic prophecies of the Old Testament. Nicholl assumes that Babylonian magi would have known the Isaian prophecies. But since it is probable that the prophecies of Second Isaiah originated in Jewish colonies in northern Arabia, Nabatean magi would have had deeper connections with Jewish prophecy and a stronger motivation to embark on the journey to Jerusalem than their Babylonian counterparts.

If our theory is correct that the Nabatean magi combined an interest in Jewish prophecy with astrology, then there should be evidence that the Nabateans were stargazers. Was astrology in fact important to the Nabateans at the time of the birth of Christ? Indeed it was, and there is amazing proof that this is so.

Nabatean Stargazers

We have already seen how the Nabatean civilization was founded during the reign of the moon-worshipping King Nabonidus in the sixth century BC. Rock carvings of Nabonidus portray him facing a star (that is, a planet) and crescent moon—astrological signs of royalty but also reminders of his devotion to the religion of the moon god Sin, a religion replete with astrological and lunar prognostications.

Ancient Middle Eastern religions all had an astral dimension, and the Nabatean religion was no exception.[30] "Astrology was not unknown to the Arabs.... [F]our of the Arabian tribes took their names from stars."[31] The followers of ancient religions watched the movements of the heavens, named their gods and goddesses after celestial bodies, and believed the movement of the planets and stars paralleled events on Earth.

The evidence suggests that Babylonian and Jewish wise men were present at the Arabian court of Nabonidus in the sixth century BC, but did their presence continue for five hundred years as the Nabatean civilization developed? Were there stargazing magi in the court of Aretas IV at the time of Christ's birth?

There are practical reasons to believe there were. The Bedouins have always been stargazers.[32] The Nabateans, voyagers and desert travelers, had, in addition to their religious interest in the stars, an economic motivation to become astronomical experts. Both the desert and the ocean were without landmarks, so for the Nabateans the stars were not only gods and goddesses but vital navigational markers.

But is there any rock-solid evidence that the Nabateans were astrologers?

There is. The new science of archaeoastronomy uses modern technology to uncover the astrological significance of ancient structures. A team of archaeoastronomers studying the temples and tombs of Petra has found that they are aligned with the seasonal equinox, suggesting a strong astrological interest in the culture of the first-century Nabateans.[33]

The main religious sites in Petra are the so-called "high places." Their hilltop perches put these shrines closer to the heavens (and

Fig. 9 Photo showing the Nabatean zodiac. *Courtesy of Wikimedia Commons.*

therefore to the gods) and facilitated celestial studies. Like Stonehenge in England, the shrines may have been used as observatories, the obelisks and standing stones functioning as fixed points with which to make astronomical calculations and astrological predictions.

A Nabatean Zodiac

There is more rock-solid evidence. Literally. Archaeologists have found carvings at Nabatean temples representing the seven planets.[34] Most importantly, in 1937 the famous American archaeologist Nelson Glueck discovered at the astrologically aligned temple of Khirbet et-Tannur[35] an amazing zodiac carved in stone and dating from the first century AD. The zodiac, half of which is in a museum in Jordan and half in Ohio, proves that the Nabateans at the time of Christ's birth were fascinated with astronomy and astrology.[36]

This zodiac, Glueck wrote, "dramatize[s] the great importance attached by the Nabateans to the heavenly firmament. They beheld in its orbs the reflections of their gods whose powers governed the mysteries of nature and the conditions of mankind during life on Earth and its continuance in the hereafter."[37]

There is an intriguing mystery about this famous Nabatean zodiac. Scholars can't understand why its star signs are in a different order than on other zodiacs. In the circular zodiac, Aries the Ram is usually placed at the lower right quadrant of the circle. In the Nabatean zodiac, however, Aries is placed at the top.

There are also two mysterious stone dots in the frame next to Aries. Might the two raised dots represent Jupiter and the moon, which were aligned in the constellation Aries at the time of Christ's birth, confirming Michael Molnar's astrological theory? Could this zodiac have actually been created by the Nabatean Magi or their followers? Did they move Aries to the top of their zodiac to indicate that after the birth of Christ all time and nature had revolved and been transformed?

Whether the zodiac from Khirbet et-Tannur is an artifact of the Nabatean Magi can never be more than speculation, but it is clear that the Nabateans were expert stargazing astrologers at the time of Christ's birth and had been for centuries.

The Nabateans' religion was fundamentally astral, and their astronomical skills and astrological capabilities most likely originated in primitive Arabian religion, the moon worship of Nabonidus, and the traditions of the Babylonian magi who had migrated to Arabia.

Enter the Greeks

There is another fascinating detail in the study of ancient astrology which points to the Nabatean identity of the Magi. Astrological studies in the ancient Middle East were shaped by two distinct traditions, the Greek and the Persian. It was Greek astrological theory that assigned the star sign Aries to Judea, an assignment that is crucial to Michael Molnar's theory about the star and does not contradict Nicholl's ideas about a unique comet.

There is no evidence that Babylonian astrologers at the time of Christ's birth were following Hellenistic astrological theories,[38] but it is very likely that Nabatean astrologers *were*. The Nabatean civilization was heavily influenced by Greek thought and culture in the decades just before the Nativity of Jesus, and this influence would have extended to astrology. Knowing the messianic prophecies from Isaiah, the Nabatean Magi were perfectly placed to predict the birth of a messianic king of the Jews when they observed Jupiter's rising in Aries.

Eastern potentates all had soothsayers and wise men as counsellors. Were the Nabatean magi part of King Aretas IV's inner circle? If so, the motivation and timing were perfect for Aretas IV to send them on a diplomatic mission to the court of Herod.

Furthermore, their trade routes took the Nabateans to the doorstep of Herod's palace in Jerusalem. The common-sense solution is always to be preferred: If the wise men were from Nabatea, they did not need a magical star to guide them through the desert.

They knew the Jewish prophecies, and they had discerned the astrological signs pointing to the birth of a king of the Jews. Herod was the king of the Jews. Something very important had taken place, and it was in the interest of their king to learn more. What better way than to make a diplomatic courtesy call? So they mounted their horses and made the comparatively short journey to Jerusalem.

All of the evidence now points to the Nabatean origins of the wise men of Bethlehem. But there is one more crucial scrap of evidence that confirms the theory, namely, what Matthew meant when he wrote that the wise men came "from the East."

CHAPTER ELEVEN

Wise Men from the East

The Magi story is unique among the stories of the New Testament in the way it developed so quickly into legend and then into fantastic myth. The influence of Gnosticism, with its fascination with mysticism and mystery, encouraged the wild embellishment of Matthew's simple account.

Also encouraging this embellishment was the supposed origin of the wise men. Because of Matthew's use of the word *magi* and because of the gnostic traditions that grew up in Armenia and Asia Minor, the early Christians naturally assumed that the wise men were members of the ancient priestly caste of magi from Persia.

The gnostics were fascinated by secret lore, arcane traditions, and supernatural flights of fancy. The idea that the wise men who traveled to worship the Christ child represented an ancient cult of priestly soothsayers suited the gnostics' obsession with all that was spectacular, supernatural, and stupendous. Thus, according to the ludicrous gnostic fantasy *The Revelation of the Magi*, the wise men were "members of an ancient mystical order and reside in a mythical land called Shir, located in the extreme east of the world at the shore of the Great Ocean."[1]

By the time the wise men had been given names, an Armenian tradition taught that Balthasar came from Arabia, Melchior from Persia, and Caspar from India.[2] The Nestorian Christians said there were twelve wise men, while medieval myths linked them with a Mongol tribe, Genghis Khan, and the legendary Central Asian Christian king, Prester John.[3] According to another elaboration, the Empress Helena miraculously discovered the tombs of the Magi in Persia. The holy relics made their way to Italy and were finally enshrined in the cathedral of Cologne.

The legends have not been limited to the Middle East. The Ethiopians said the Magi came from East Africa, Chinese Christians claimed the wise men were from China, the esoteric writer George Gurdjieff taught that they were ancient Asian occult masters,[4] and the guru Paramahansa Yogananda boasted that the wise men were "great sages of India."[5]

Wise Men of History or Mystery?

Modern Christians still assume details that are simply not present in the short account in Matthew's gospel, accepting the traditions that the Magi were three kings named Balthasar, Melchior, and Caspar, that they traveled in a camel caravan from a distant eastern land, guided by a miraculous star, and that the objective of their journey was to worship the newborn Messiah as the Son of God. While they may not accept the ornate gnostic embellishments, their understanding has been colored by centuries of legend and myth for which there is no evidence.

Consequently, academics have been skeptical about the historicity of the Magi story. Raymond Brown describes how, in the early days of modern Biblical scholarship, disbelief in the historical Magi validated one's scholarly credentials.[6] A Biblical scholar of our generation has assured me that the same is true today. "Suggesting that the Magi story might have a historical basis is a no-fly zone," he explains, "If you want a career in New Testament scholarship that's somewhere you just don't go."

Brown was one of the scholars who at least allowed that there might be a historical basis to the story of the Magi, offering three options for the origin of the magi: Persia-Parthia, Babylon, and Arabia. He was one of the few to take the historical possibility seriously, for which he is to be commended. The fact is that scholars have not done their homework. When confronted with the question of where the Magi may have come from, they simply repeat the assumption that the Magi were from Persia. With no further research, they reflexively assert that if such characters really made a journey to Bethlehem, then they came from Persia and were members of the ancient caste of Zoroastrian priests.

Then with no further examination of the evidence, they move on quickly. The most recent scholarly work on the question of the star, for example, is the voluminous book of essays *The Star of Bethlehem and the Magi*, edited by the New Testament scholar George van Kooten and the astrophysicist Peter Barthel. They are certainly not scholarly slouches, but along with the rest of the distinguished academics who contributed to the volume, they assume that the Magi were Persian-Parthians. Why assume this when all the evidence we have examined—political, religious, and cultural—points compellingly to Nabatea as the home of the Magi?

There is additional evidence, in fact, that completes the picture, allowing us to conclude that the wise men were indeed diplomats from the Nabatean court of King Aretas IV. It is found in Matthew's little phrase "wise men came from the East."

Wise Men from the East

In AD 70, under the command of Titus, the Romans finally put down the long-running Jewish rebellion. After a long siege, the great temple that Herod had built was destroyed, and Jerusalem was leveled. The followers of Jesus, along with the rest of the Jews, were scattered. Naturally they fled to cities where Christian communities had already been established.

The historian Eusebius records that the Christians fled across the Jordan River and north to the city of Pella.[7] Damascus and Antioch were also centers where fellow Christians were ready to welcome them. The New Testament records that Christian churches were established not only in Rome itself but also in the Greek cities of Corinth, Thessalonica, and Ephesus, as well as the cities of Galatia and Colossae in Asia Minor (present-day Turkey).

Mathew's gospel was probably written to Jews in Judea before the fall of Jerusalem in AD 70. As the Jewish-Christian believers fled the war zone, however, the new religion became centered in Asia Minor, Greece, and Italy. When the next generation of Christians read in Matthew's gospel that "magi from the East came to Jerusalem," they naturally drew the conclusion that they came from Parthia. If you lived in Asia Minor, Greece, or Rome, the "East," obviously, was not Arabia but the kingdom of Parthia.

Matthew's Magi?

That Matthew called the visitors "magi" made it seem even more obvious that the wise men came from Persia. After all, the word originated with the famous Persian sect of priestly court advisors. The combination of "magi" and "from the East" pointed to an easy solution: The wise men who came to pay homage to the Christ child must have been magi from Persia.

As in most mystery stories, however, the easy, quick solution is rarely the correct one.

One mustn't give too much weight to Matthew's use of the Greek word *magoi*. It may refer to the famous Persian sect of Zoroastrian priests, but it is also used in the Bible and in secular literature of the time for any type of magician, wise man, dream-teller, or astrologer. Mathieu Ossendrijver, a historian of ancient science, observes, "In some sources from the Greco-Roman period 'magi' is used in a much wider sense, as a generic term for non-Greek scholars."[8] Raymond Brown agrees: "The term *magi* refers to those engaged in occult arts and covers a wide range of astronomers, fortune tellers, priestly augurers, and magicians of varying plausibility."[9]

Tony Maalouf, outlining the various uses of the word in the New Testament and the secular literature of the time, concludes that "the word can be used to refer to persons other than Persians.... [I]t was applied to Jews and to Aramaic easterners."[10] Because the word is used for magicians, soothsayers, and astrologers in other cultures, it is unlikely that Matthew is identifying the wise men specifically as the Persian magi. So Maalouf concludes, "In Matthew the word *magoi* is most probably used in the neutral sense, referring to seekers of science, wisdom, and knowledge."[11]

If we are correct that the Greek version of Matthew's gospel is based on an older Aramaic-Hebrew collection of sayings and stories, the case for a generic reading of "magi" is even stronger. The Aramaic word for the wise men, *m'gushai*, does not refer specifically to *Persian* magi but to magicians or wise men in general.[12]

In fact, wise men were common in practically every culture across the ancient Middle East.[13] Every king had his band of astrologers, priests, soothsayers, necromancers, and interpreters of dreams.[14] The historian Pliny, for example, tells how the philosophers Pythagoras and Democritus learned from magi in different parts of the ancient world: "Both of these...had visited the magi of Persia, Arabia, Ethiopia, and Egypt."[15]

By the time of the Greek empire, the Persian magi, because of both persecution and their missionary endeavors, had spread far beyond their home territory. One Zoroastrian document from the Achaemenid period, for example, asks the faithful to pray for the magi as they "go from afar to those who seek righteousness in the lands."[16] Jean Danié-lou, a scholar of the early Church, writes, "We know that at the beginning of the Christian era there were Iranian magi all over the Middle East, especially in Syria."[17] By the time Matthew was writing, therefore, the Greek word *magoi* could refer to magi of Babylonian origin who had been dispersed or to a sage, astrologer, or soothsayer from almost any contemporary culture.

Where Is the East?

Another indication that Matthew was not referring specifically to Persian-Parthian magi is his statement that the wise men "came from the East." Christians in Asia Minor, Greece, and Rome would have taken "East" to refer to Persia-Parthia and beyond, but they were not Matthew's audience. He was writing for the first Jewish Christians, who lived in Judea and Syria.[18]

If you are in Judea or Syria, the "East" is not Persia-Parthia but Arabia.

Tony Maalouf, arguing that the "east" for Matthew's audience was northern Arabia,[19] makes the point that first-century residents of Palestine traveling to Persia-Parthia had to go north first and then east, and he cites several Old Testament references to the Babylonians and Assyrians as "people of the north." Furthermore, in the Old Testament the "armies and kings coming from Persia or Babylon to the Holy Land were never mentioned with the connotation of 'coming from the east.'"[20] He concludes that "the 'east' direction (*qedem*) is for the Palestinian Jew a technical term referring to the Syro-Arabian Desert."[21]

"That there might be magi or wise men among [the Arabian tribes] would not be surprising, for they had a reputation for wisdom."[22] This is supported by references in the early church writers Justin Martyr, Tertullian, Epiphanius, and Eusebius to the "land of the East" as the territory of the Arabian descendants of Abraham.[23]

In the Talmud, Margaret Barker writes, the east "for legal purposes was defined as beyond Rekem, probably Petra."[24]

The Biblical scholar James Montgomery agrees that "this name, Kedem, i.e., East, can only be explained from a Palestinian point of view, and the region must have lain east of Palestine. And it lay in the so-called desert, the Roman Arabia Deserta."[25] Maalouf also quotes the French New Testament scholar R. P. P. Benoit: "The 'east' where [the Magi] came from designates without doubt the regions of Arabia which stretch east of the Jordan river and the Dead Sea."[26]

Furthermore, in the Old Testament "the people of the East" was the term used most frequently for nomadic Arabs. The New Testament scholar C. W. Briggs writes, "In the Old Testament literature, Arabia was often referred to as 'Kedem,' *the East*.... Trained in Palestine, Paul naturally used 'the East' and 'Arabia' as interchangeable terms."[27] Philip K. Hitti, a historian of Arabia, explains the Hebrew terminology. "'Qedem' and 'Bene Qedem' of the Old Testament, rendered in the English versions... 'east', 'children of the east', 'people of the east', etc.,...mean the land and the Bedouins east of Palestine; in general, Arabia and the Arabians.... The 'wise men from the east' (Matt. 2:1), therefore, who followed the star to Jerusalem were possibly Bedouins from the North Arabian desert rather than Magi from Persia."[28]

The Earliest Evidence of the East

What did the first Christians believe about the true identity of the Magi? We have seen that the gnostic Christians in Asia Minor and Armenia latched on to the idea that the wise men were exotic Persian magicians, and because of this, the tradition in the West that the Magi were from Persia or India took root firmly within the first five centuries of the Christian tradition.

The Magi were famously portrayed in Persian-Parthian costume in the mosaics of the emperor Justinian's church in Ravenna, and when the same emperor rebuilt the basilica in Bethlehem in AD 565, they were similarly depicted. When armies from Persia invaded Bethlehem in AD 614, they spared the basilica because they recognized their national costume in the mosaics of the wise men.[29]

The tradition that the wise men came from Persia was supported not only by the early extra-Biblical gnostic texts and the sixth-century mosaics but also by some of the early Christian writers called the "Apostolic Fathers." Saint Clement of Alexandria (d. AD 215) is the earliest Father to ascribe Persian origins to the Magi, and Saint Cyril of Alexandria (d. AD 444), Saint Maximus the Confessor (d. AD 662), and Theodotus of Ancyra (d. *circa* AD 445) all agree with him.

However, the most intriguing witness from the early church appears a good fifty years before Clement of Alexandria. Justin Martyr was born in Samaria, just north of Judea, around the year AD 100 and was therefore writing fewer than a hundred years after the death and resurrection of Jesus Christ. Like Matthew himself, Justin wrote from the early Christian heartland, where he was close to the traditions about Jesus that had been passed down among the first Christians—the same traditions from which Matthew's gospel is derived.

Justin's account of an argument with a Jew named Trypho includes the following phrases:

> For, at the time of His birth, the Magi came from Arabia and worshipped Him....
> At the time the Magi came from Arabia to King Herod and said....
> Now, these Magi from Arabia came to Bethlehem, worshipped the child, and presented to Him gifts of gold, frankincense and myrrh....
> There the Arabian Magi found Him....
> Now when the Arabian Magi failed to return to Herod....[30]

Fifty years later, in North Africa, Tertullian (d. AD 220) deduced from the three gifts that the wise men came from Damascus and

Arabia.[31] An even earlier witness, Clement of Rome (d. AD 99), also identified the region of the "East," the source of frankincense and myrrh, with Arabia. About the year AD 95, comparing Christ to the phoenix of Greek mythology, Clement wrote, "For, in the regions of the east, that is, the vicinity of Arabia…there is a bird which is named the phoenix…. [W]hen the time of its dissolution and death arrives it makes for itself a nest of frankincense and myrrh…. [I]t then makes its way from the country of Arabia to Egypt."[32]

Finally, the church historian Epiphanius of Salamis (d. AD 403), writing from Cyprus, believed the Magi were from the northern Arabian tribe of Keturah, which, like the other northern Arabian tribes, was descended from the patriarch Abraham.[33]

Tony Maalouf observes that Epiphanius, Tertullian, and Justin Martyr traced their belief in the Arabian origin of the Magi independently of one another and from different sources. He concludes that "the best way to account for the similarities and differences among these church fathers is to see that Justin, Tertullian, and Epiphanius were all depending on an earlier eastern tradition that referred to Arabia, without further specification as the origin of these wise men."[34]

Although the tradition that the wise men originated in Persia became dominant in the Western church, when we take Matthew's textual evidence at face value and consider his Jewish audience and Judean provenance, we can conclude that for Matthew's readers the "East" was obviously the Nabatean territory of Arabia. When we add the early testimony of Justin Martyr and the other Apostolic Fathers, the conclusion that the wise men came from northern Arabia becomes unavoidable.

Nabateans or Not?

If this is true, why didn't Matthew say that the wise men were Nabateans?

Because he didn't need to.

His audience were Jews from Judea. They knew the Nabateans well. Herod the Great's mother was a Nabatean princess. Herod's son Antipas married the daughter of the Nabatean king Aretas IV. For Matthew's audience the "East" was synonymous with northern Arabia. When an American refers to the "South," everyone knows he means the southeastern United States. Likewise, when Matthew said the wise men came from the "East," it would have been obvious to his readers that the wise men were magi-type counselors from the court of Aretas IV.

It was only as the Christian church moved north and west and became more Gentile than Jewish that the simple meaning of the "East" was forgotten. It was Gentile Christians in Asia Minor, Greece, and Rome who did not understand the true origins of the wise men, concluding mistakenly that they were magi from Persia.

Biblical scholars and Christian believers have been making the same mistake for the past two thousand years.

Nevertheless, Matthew's language in the story of the Magi is somewhat obscure. He writes of "wise men from the East" who "returned to their own country by a different route." If he knew they were Nabateans, why not say so and mention the Nabatean king, Aretas IV? Was Matthew being elusive on purpose? Was there a good reason why Matthew kept the identity of the wise men somewhat shrouded?

I believe there was a good reason, and it has to do not only with Matthew and the Magi but also the very foundation of the Christian church and the monumental figure of Saint Paul.

CHAPTER TWELVE

What Happened to the Wise Men?

Using what we have discovered, it is time to read again the simple story of the Magi from Matthew's gospel. We are going to set aside all the lovely, traditional details we have come to take for granted and read the account on its own with only the discoveries from this book to illuminate the story.

To help with this, I have interposed my own commentary into the text.

> *After Jesus was born in Bethlehem in Judea, during the time of King Herod,*

For complicated reasons the date of Jesus' birth is debated, but the historian Josephus records that an eclipse took place the month of Herod the Great's death. That eclipse can be dated to 4 BC, so most scholars conclude that the birth of Jesus took place between 6 and 4 BC.

Bethlehem is a small town about six miles south of Jerusalem.

Magi from the East came to Jerusalem

Matthew uses the word "magi" in a general way, meaning any kind of shaman, astrologer, prophet, soothsayer, or wise man. Sapient courtiers were commonplace in the ancient world, and magi of Babylonian origin were known to be dispersed across Asia Minor, Syria, Arabia, and Egypt.

"The East" in the Old Testament and among the Jews in Judea and Syria (to whom Matthew was writing) was understood to be Arabia. The Nabatean kingdom of Aretas IV was the Arabian power at the time, therefore Matthew's Magi were Nabateans.

The capital of the Nabatean kingdom was Petra—about three hundred miles southeast of Jerusalem. The Nabatean's trade route to the port of Gaza ran about ninety miles south of Jerusalem. Their route north ran east of the Dead Sea to Damascus.

There is no mention in the gospel of a long desert trek. For Nabatean diplomats riding swift Arabian horses (not camels), the journey to Jerusalem would have been relatively short. It takes about twenty-four hours to travel one hundred miles on horseback, so it was a three- to five-day journey.

and asked, "Where is the one who has been born king of the Jews?

Herod was old and dying. The Nabateans, who had a shared ancestry with the neighboring Jews, had a cultural, historical, and religious interest in any newborn heir to Herod.

Because their trade routes to the port of Gaza went through Herod's territory, they also had an economic interest in who would be the next king.

At the time, Herod was in favor with the emperor Caesar Augustus, while the Nabatean king, Aretas IV, was not. Aretas therefore also had a political motive to please Herod and an interest in the Herodian succession.

We saw his star when it rose

They saw a remarkable comet, but they also predicted rare conjunctions of planets which, through astrological interpretation, they understood to indicate the birth of a great king to the Jews.

Familiar with Zoroastrian and Jewish prophecies, they were also watching and waiting for the prophesied Messiah.

Matthew does not say a magical star guided them on their journey. This is a later, gnostic elaboration of the story.

and have come to worship him."

They came to pay him homage because their king, Aretas IV, was building an alliance with Herod. Paying homage to a newborn prince with rich gifts was the traditional royal protocol. It was also the perfect step to build goodwill with Herod.

The ancients believed kings were divine, and knowing the prophecies, the Nabatean Magi were also intent on paying homage to the child who might be the divinely promised Messiah. "Worship," should be understood to mean "pay him homage."

When King Herod heard this he was disturbed, and all Jerusalem with him.

Famously paranoid, Herod was anxious to exterminate anyone who threatened his throne. The Magi's question on its own would have been enough to raise his suspicions. Their coming from his traditional enemy the Nabateans raised his suspicions further. What were they up to? Were these courtiers spies for King Aretas?

Herod had just had two of his sons killed for plotting against him. Was this another plot? Was there a newborn grandson of one of his murdered sons whom he didn't know about? Who was the mother? Was her family scheming to usurp his throne? Were the Nabateans ready to throw their support behind this upstart?

The Magi may have arrived with an impressive entourage and military escort. No doubt the gossip mill started up and the rumors about the visitors from the court of Aretas spread throughout the city.

> When he had called together all the people's chief priests
> and teachers of the law, he asked them where the Messiah
> was to be born.

Herod knew the prophecies of a coming Messiah, as did everyone from Roman poets to Persian priests. Aretas had sent his wise men, but they didn't have all the necessary information, so Herod called on his own wise men.

> "In Bethlehem in Judea," they replied, "for this is what the
> prophet has written:
> "'But you, Bethlehem, in the land of Judah,
> are by no means least among the rulers of Judah;
> for out of you will come a ruler
> who will shepherd my people Israel.'"
> Then Herod called the Magi secretly and found out from
> them the exact time the star had appeared.

Without knowing exactly what the astrological signs were, it is difficult to ascertain the exact dates. As we've seen in chapter ten the various theories of the conjunction of planets and the appearance of a comet all take pace around 7–6 BC.

Given the various and contradictory signs, a possible delay in the Magi's journey, and other variables, Herod, to be on the safe side, would need to exterminate all the children two years old and younger.

> *He sent them to Bethlehem and said, "Go and search care-*
> *fully for the child. As soon as you find him, report to me,*
> *so that I too may go and worship him."*
> *After they had heard the king, they went on their way,*

The Magi would have known the way to Bethlehem because they were familiar with the territory. In fact, if they had traveled north from their customary trade route, they would have passed Bethlehem on the way to Jerusalem.

> *and the star they had seen when it rose went ahead of them*
> *until it stopped over the place where the child was.*

On their short journey south, Jupiter seemed to move backward and then stop—the retrogression and stationary movement described by Molnar, Larson, and others.

We can surmise that Jupiter, instead of hovering over the place where Jesus was, appeared to move backward and stopped at the same time that the Magi were approaching Bethlehem, thus confirming their quest. Molnar discovered that Jupiter made this stationing around December 19, 6 BC.

"Stopping over the place where the child was" may be an exaggeration of what took place, or it may indicate Matthew's incomplete understanding of the astrological terminology. On the other hand, if Nicholl and Humphreys are correct, the tail of the unique comet shone down on the very house where Mary and the child were.

When they saw the star, they were overjoyed.

The Magi were overjoyed because, according to Ptolemy's theory of astrology, the retrogression and stationary movement of planets strengthened and confirmed the predictions that had been made.

On coming to the house, they saw the child with his mother Mary

The wise men came to a house, not a stable. Mary and Joseph, therefore, must have moved into better accommodations. The Magi apparently did not arrive immediately after Christ's birth, for the word "child" means "toddler" when translated.

If the journey only took four or five days, the question arises why the Magi were delayed in their arrival. We don't know. Astrology is imprecise. It could be that they misinterpreted the star signs or that they were confused about the timing. It could be that Aretas IV delayed their trip for political reasons. Maybe they were waiting for other details of their predictions or other political players to fall into place.

and they bowed down and paid him homage.

"Paying homage" indicates the political nature of their visit. The Nabatean Magi were on a diplomatic courtesy call from the court of Aretas to the court of Herod, but they were familiar with the prophecies, so there was also a religious dimension to their homage.

Then they opened their treasures and presented him with gifts of gold, frankincense, and myrrh.

There is no mention of the number of wise men or that they were kings. These traditions accumulated later.

The gifts of gold, frankincense, and myrrh, commodities widely known as representative of the Nabatean nation, confirm the Magi's origin in Arabia.

Although they were not themselves kings, the wise men were diplomatic envoys from the court of Aretas IV, so the royal dignity that tradition has conferred on them is not completely misplaced.

> *And having been warned in a dream not to go back to Herod,*

This does not demand a supernatural interpretation. Many people experience premonitions in dreams. It is perfectly plausible that the Magi, knowing Herod's bloodthirsty ways and paranoid nature, had a bad dream about him.

> *they returned to their country by another route.*

Matthew seems deliberately vague. He is also seems somewhat cagey when he says they "came from the East." It could be that his source provided only limited information. If Herod felt threatened, however, by the diplomats from Aretas's court and was angry that they had disobeyed him, he would have alerted Aretas and had him apprehend the Magi on their return. We may speculate, therefore, that Matthew's source obscured the Magi's identity and destination out of fear that they might be persecuted by Herod and Aretas.

Where did the Magi go? Instead of heading back to Jerusalem, they may have sought refuge in Damascus, traveling east and then north around the Dead Sea and joining the Nabatean trade route that ran north from Petra to Damascus.

Tradition confirms the beginning of this route. Between Bethlehem and the Dead Sea is the ancient monastery of Mar Saba. A smaller monastery on that road, dedicated to Saint Theodosius, is built on the site of a cave in which, ancient tradition says, the Magi stopped on their journey from Bethlehem.[1]

The city of Damascus had been part of the Nabatean kingdom under King Aretas III, but at the time of Christ's birth it was under the control of the Romans. If the Magi sheltered in Damascus, therefore, they would have been "in their own country" and yet safe from both Herod and Aretas.

The Damascus Connection

Up till now we have tried to piece together the facts about the Magi. Now, admittedly, we are speculating. Why should we imagine that the Magi took refuge in Damascus? There are intriguing clues that they not only went to Damascus but also were involved in the theological developments in the decades before Jesus' ministry and afterward—clues linked to the Dead Sea Scrolls and the Jewish sect called the Essenes.

A strict and celibate monastic group, the Essenes were deeply interested in apocalyptic and Messianic prophecies. Because they were persecuted by the other Jews, the Essenes were scattered across Judea. They "lived in 'large numbers in every town,' [according to Josephus] and had a network to support members when they travelled."[2]

The Essenes were most probably the community that was established at Qumran and were therefore guardians of the library now known as the Dead Sea Scrolls. As we saw in chapter seven, the community at Qumran was on the border of the Nabatean territory. And I suggested that the Nabatean wise men would have known of the Essenes and been familiar with the book of the prophet Isaiah—one of the great finds among the Dead Sea Scrolls.

Another of the Dead Sea Scrolls, known as the Damascus Document, sets out the rules for a religious community and recounts the history of the Jewish sect (presumably the Essenes) who went north into exile in Damascus because of persecution. The eminent church historian Jean Daniélou proposed that the Essenes there met magi who influenced their thought, a meeting that played a part in the development of early Christianity.[3]

Daniélou's speculation raises some fascinating questions. Tertullian hints that the Magi were from Damascus,[4] and in a difficult passage, Justin Martyr also links the Magi to Damascus.[5] When might the Magi have met Essenes in Damascus? Was it after the Magi visited Bethlehem? Some scholars believe the Essenes abandoned Qumran after being persecuted by Herod and settled at the castle of Kokhba, southwest of Damascus, after which some returned to Qumran.[6]

The tradition that the Magi stopped between Bethlehem and the Dead Sea takes them in the direction of the Qumran community, which was on the west coast of the Dead Sea. Could it be that the Magi took refuge from Herod and Aretas IV with the Essenes, whom they already knew, at Qumran before heading north to shelter with the Essenes occupying the castle of Kokhba near Damascus? Again, these are guesses based on hints of tradition.

The Irish Biblical scholar Jerome Murphy-O'Connor thought the Essenes were influenced by Babylonian religion.[7] The Babylonian influences he discerned may have come from contact with Nabatean Magi, whose wisdom was rooted in Babylonian lore.

Did the Nabatean Magi settle in Damascus with the Essenes and establish a school of wisdom there in the years after Christ's birth? Reflecting Nabatean history and culture, did that school of wisdom blend Eastern religion with the ancient Arabian-Abrahamic strand of Judaism and Greek philosophy? Did the Magi, pondering what had happened, begin to understand the birth of the child in Bethlehem to be the fulfillment of both Isaiah's prophecies and the other more ancient aspects of their religion?

The speculation becomes even more intriguing when we move forward about thirty years from the birth of Christ to the events after his death and resurrection.

The Apostle Paul and Arabia

If Jesus was crucified around the year AD 30, then by AD 32 the future apostle Paul, still known as Saul, must have been acting as an agent for the Pharisees in the persecution of the first Christians, arresting, imprisoning, and killing the followers of this new sect.[8]

In the ninth chapter of the Acts of the Apostles, Luke recounts how Saul received letters from the Jewish leaders in Jerusalem authorizing him to travel to Damascus to round up the "followers of the Way." On the road he experienced a vision of Jesus Christ and was converted. After spending a few days in Damascus, he went to Jerusalem and met the apostles.

But this is not the order of events that Paul himself gives elsewhere.

When writing to the Galatian Christians, Paul refers to his miraculous conversion and says, "I want you to know, brothers and sisters, that the gospel I preached is not of human origin. I did not receive it from any man, nor was I taught it; rather, I received it by revelation from Jesus Christ."

He then remembers how he persecuted the church: "For you have heard of my previous way of life in Judaism, how intensely I persecuted the church of God and tried to destroy it. I was advancing in Judaism beyond many of my own age among my people and was extremely zealous for the traditions of my fathers."

Then he explains what happened after his conversion, "But when God…was pleased to reveal his Son in me so that I might preach him among the Gentiles, my immediate response was not to consult any human being. I did not go up to Jerusalem to see those who were apostles before I was, but I went into Arabia. Later I returned to Damascus. Then after three years, I went up to Jerusalem to get acquainted with Peter and stayed with him fifteen days." (Galatians 1:11–18)

Why was Paul so intent on rooting out the believers in Damascus? Was it because there was an important cell of believers already established there? Was it because the community of disciples Paul met after his conversion had already been in Damascus for the past thirty years? Had that community been established by the fugitive Magi after their life-changing visit to Bethlehem?

Daniélou mentions an ancient tradition that Paul was converted at Castle Kokhba,[9] the name of which means "Star Tower." If there is truth to the ancient tradition, then Paul was blinded by a radiant light at Kokhba, which means "star." Was his sudden illumination seen as a sign of direct divine revelation similar to the star that had led the Magi to Christ?

Immediately after his conversion Paul went into Arabia for three years. What prompted him to do that? His sojourn in Arabia has mystified scholars.[10] Some suggest he went there to begin his missionary work,[11] but this seems unlikely so soon after his sudden conversion. Others suggest that he went into Arabia for a meditative retreat, like Jesus' forty days in the wilderness.[12]

The New Testament scholar Margaret Barker observes, "After his conversion, Paul went to Arabia, and his visit may help to identify the magi. He came back better informed about his new faith and able to explain that Christianity was rooted in something older than the law of Moses. Who instructed him?"[13]

In the intervening years, had the Magi returned to Nabatea to establish a school of wisdom that wove together Babylonian wisdom, the ancient Abrahamic strain of Judaism, and Greek philosophy? As Paul was called to be a missionary to the Gentiles, did he and his mentors in Damascus consider it essential for him to understand this synthesis so that he might effectively preach the Christian message? Speculating about the presence of Magian-Essene settlements in Arabia, Barker asks, "Did Paul receive instruction from them about his new faith? These questions cannot be answered, but the evidence suggests they should be asked."[14]

Paul and the Magian School

Anyone who reads the New Testament must be astonished by the theology of Paul. His epistles date from about the year AD 49 to just before his death in the mid-60s, but the Acts of the Apostles indicates that he was actively preaching before the composition of the letters. His astounding understanding of Jesus Christ developed extraordinarily quickly.

Paul came to understand that this wandering rabbi—a crucified political prisoner—was the Second Adam, the cosmic Christ, the one in whom the fullness of God dwells in bodily form (Colossians 2:9), and before whom everything in heaven and Earth bows down (Ephesians 1:10). Where did these ideas come from? Some of them must have been the fruit of the excellent Jewish education Paul received in the school of Gamaliel (Acts 22:3), but his theology includes far more than traditional Judaism. It expands Judaism from the inside out, eventually bursting out of it.

We find in Paul's theology a synthesis of the same three cultural and religious strains that we find in the Nabateans. The first strain is Abrahamic Judaism. This is the Judaism from before the destruction of Solomon's temple by Nebuchadnezzar in 586 BC. The Arabian tribes claimed descent from Abraham, and Nabatean religion had its roots in the earlier Abrahamic religion. This earlier form of Judaism was also the religion of the Jewish refugees who fled into Arabia in the sixth century BC.

The second strain in Paul's theology is the mystery religions that had grown out of Mesopotamian culture and were the second source of Nabatean culture and religion. Paul warns his followers of the dangers of mystery religions, but he also uses the language and imagery of the mystery religions, correcting them and using them to point to the mystery of redemption in Jesus Christ.

Paul also understands Greek philosophy, which he integrates successfully into his theology. The Nabateans had also absorbed and integrated elements of Greek culture, religion, and philosophy.

Somewhere and somehow, Paul learned how these three elements could be fused to explain the gospel of Jesus Christ to a non-Jewish audience. Did he develop his theology during his three years in Arabia and Damascus? Who were his teachers? Did Paul learn from a school of Nabatean wise men? Was he taught by the Magi themselves?

The Magian Gospel of Paul

It would require an entire book by a better theologian and Biblical scholar than I will ever be to show in detail how Abrahamic Judaism, Babylonian mystery religion, and Greek philosophy are woven together in Paul's theology, but I can provide a few hints and pointers.

One of the predominant themes in Paul's thought is the correction of a Judaism that is only concerned with the law of Moses.[15] In the third chapter of his epistle to the Galatians, Paul emphasizes that God's promise was to Abraham through faith and not through the law, and he says that those who have faith in Christ are children of Abraham. In Galatians 4:25, Paul compares Abraham's concubine, the slave girl Hagar, to those enslaved by the law that was given at Sinai. (Paul comments in passing that Sinai is in Arabia, a hint, perhaps, that his theology was influenced by his stay in Arabia.) Those who have faith in Christ, on the other hand, are free like Abraham's wife, Sarah.

Throughout his writings Paul speaks of this clash with great fervor. He does not reject the Mosaic understanding, but he balances it by referring back to Abraham. The foundation of the Jewish religion is the covenant of faith that was established with Abraham and his descendants. Margaret Barker suggests that this Abrahamic religion was considered the original by the refugees from the destruction of Jerusalem and that they considered the legalistic religion that emerged after the exile to be an illicit development. As we have seen in chapter five, these refugees were established in Jewish settlements across Arabia.

The second aspect that Paul integrates into his theology is the mystery religions of the East. Gnostic mystery religions, like New Age religions today, were a mixture of esoteric teaching, fascination with angels, cosmic knowledge, heavenly hierarchies, and arcane wisdom. Paul condemns these false teachers throughout his writings, but he also uses the imagery and language of mystery to explain the death and resurrection of Jesus.

So he writes to the Ephesians about God's revelation: "With all wisdom and understanding, he made known to us the mystery of his will according to his good pleasure, which he purposed in Christ, to be put into effect when the times reach their fulfillment—to bring unity to all things in heaven and on earth under Christ" (Ephesians 1:9). He writes of God's mysterious plan, which was hidden from the foundation of the Earth, "His intent was that now, through the church, the manifold wisdom of God should be made known to the rulers and authorities in the heavenly realms, according to his eternal purpose that he accomplished in Christ Jesus our Lord" (Ephesians 3:10).

Paul reclaims the mystery religions' dualistic language when he writes, "For you were once darkness, but now you are light in the Lord. Live as children of light (for the fruit of the light consists in all goodness, righteousness and truth) and find out what pleases the Lord. Have nothing to do with the fruitless deeds of darkness, but rather expose them. It is shameful even to mention what the disobedient do in secret." (Ephesians 5:8–12)

Throughout his epistle to the Ephesians, he refers to the "great mystery" of the faith and urges his followers to engage in the cosmic battle between good and evil: "For our struggle is not against flesh and blood, but against the rulers, against the authorities, against the powers of this dark world and against the spiritual forces of evil in the heavenly realms" (Ephesians 6:12).

Paul has a genius for using pagan imagery and terminology to preach the Christian gospel, but his borrowing of non-Jewish material is not confined to the mystery religions.[16] He also reclaims and reinterprets the philosophy of the Greeks. In his first epistle to the Corinthians he stands the concept of philosophy on its head with his declaration that the cross of Christ is true wisdom: "For Jews demand signs and Greeks desire wisdom, but we proclaim Christ crucified, a stumbling block to Jews and foolishness to Gentiles, but to those who are the called, both Jews and Greeks, Christ the power of God and the wisdom of God" (Corinthians 1:22–25). Adeptly preaching to a philosophical audience at the Areopagus in Athens (Acts 17:22–34), Paul uses their own terminology and imagery to present his message.[17]

Matthew, Luke, and Paul

As in any investigation, the answers one finds produce more questions. If my theory is correct, and the wise men from Matthew's gospel are Nabatean diplomats from the court of Aretas IV, then why didn't Matthew say so? There are three reasons.

First, Matthew didn't need to be more specific. As we have seen in chapter eleven, his audience of Jewish Christians in Judea would have understood clearly who the Magi were. "The East" for them was shorthand for Nabatea. But his terseness might also be a result of his sources. The Magi story would have been one of the earliest of the oral traditions on which Matthew relied, and he may have received only the bare bones of the story himself.

Second, the story may have been passed down in such a spare form because the first disciples—Matthew's sources—were aware that the Magi were fugitives. Both Herod and Aretas IV were known for their vengeful and paranoid cruelty. It could be that Matthew was protecting the Magi by using deliberately vague language. The continued persecution of the Magian school might explain Aretas IV's desire to capture Paul in Damascus[18] and the slowness of Christianity to take root in the Nabatean kingdom.

Third, and most importantly, as Daniélou points out, Matthew's audience was the early Christians of Judea and Syria.[19] There was conflict even then with false magicians and Eastern gnostic sects.[20] The Nabatean Magi would have been suspect to the staid Jewish authorities, and the ruling Pharisees had persecuted the Essenes. If the Magi and Essenes were influential in the nascent Christian community in Damascus, then it was important for them that Matthew validate the benign Magian influence by including the wise men in his gospel, but the less said the better.

One also wonders why Luke, the companion of Paul, did not mention the Magi story. If Paul learned his theology in a Magian school of wisdom in Damascus and Arabia, wouldn't Luke have known about the Magi, and wouldn't it have been natural for him to mention them in his account of the birth of Christ?

It could be that Luke did not know the Magi story because he did not have Matthew's original collection of Hebrew-Aramaic stories and sayings as one of his sources. It is more likely, however, that Luke knew of the Magi story but deliberately omitted it, just as he omitted the detail of Paul's sojourn in Arabia in his account of Paul's conversion in the Acts of the Apostles. Why would he do that?

Because Paul was an outsider. Paul's account of the first years after his conversion in the epistle to the Galatians bristles with a sense of conflict with the other apostles and the Jerusalem church. Luke portrays Paul's relationship with the other apostles much more sympathetically than Paul himself does. It would make sense, then, for him to weed out the references to the Magi's visit and to Paul's tutelage in Arabia to placate the Jewish Christians, who would have been offended by the semi-pagan Nabatean influence.

Luke would also have removed references to the Arabian Magi to improve Paul's relationship with the other Apostles. Already suspicious of Paul, they would have been more uneasy if they had known that he developed his theology outside their authority, under the guidance of theologically and culturally questionable Nabateans.

I believe this study shows beyond a reasonable doubt that the Magi of Matthew's gospel were historical figures. Whether I have all the details right remains to be seen. Whether Paul developed his theology in a Magian school of wisdom in Damascus and

Arabia will remain a matter of speculation—some will no doubt say, "wild speculation!"

Nevertheless, I hope this speculation will serve as a springboard for further discussion, debate, research, and discovery. If my theory is proved wrong, then the pursuit of truth will have been furthered, and that's a good thing. If my theory is plausible, then better scholars and historians than I can research further, and in that way the pursuit of truth will also be furthered.

In any case, the details of the birth of Jesus Christ will continue to be an absorbing mystery. The search for further understanding will require others to set out, as I have done, on a fascinating journey of discovery.

With a bit of guidance from above and with confidence in the knowledge already acquired, they can set out as the wise men did, knowing that the end of the search is a deeper understanding of the mysterious child of Bethlehem.

Why Does It Matter?

The quest for the identity of the Magi has been an absorbing passion of mine for the past couple of years. Often when I was waxing enthusiastic about my discoveries, I would notice that all too familiar glazed look in my listener's eyes, telling me that my eager interest in the Magi was not shared. I was becoming like that boring uncle most families have who is an expert in Civil War battles, the Russian royal family, train timetables, family genealogies, or the persecution of the Albigensians.

Does it really matter who the three wise men were? If they existed at all, it was a long time ago in a galaxy far, far away, right? And does it really matter if they were Persians named Balthasar, Melchior, and Caspar? Isn't it just fine to believe they came from India, China, and

Africa? Who cares? Furthermore, some Christian friends were uncomfortable with my findings. One friend, learning that the Magi probably rode horses from Petra to Jerusalem, joked, "Do I have to remove the camels from my Nativity set?" Another friend heard my theories and simply said, "I like the other version better."

I am sympathetic to their mild complaints. Yes, you can still have your camels, your long spiritual quest, and your mystical, magical star. By all means keep the school Nativity play, the "Little Drummer Boy," and "We Three Kings of Orient Are." But you should realize these are elaborations of the historical story from Matthew's gospel. They are delightful and meaningful, but they are related to the facts of Jesus' birth in the same way that the Broadway musical *Camelot* is related to the historical King Arthur.

Does it matter who the Magi were and where they came from? Yes. It matters because for too long, too many Biblical scholars have insisted that the stories of the New Testament are either fanciful elaborations of simple narratives or completely fictional accounts concocted to make Jesus more special. The Magi story has long been regarded as the one story which is most amazingly fabulous and therefore simply untrue. Scholars have debunked it and dismissed it out of hand.

Why does this matter? Because the scholars write the books and teach the classes in seminaries, Bible colleges, and theology departments around the world. They teach the men and women who are training to be ministers, priests, pastors, catechists, and religion teachers. Several generations of religious leaders have now been taught that the Magi story is mythical make-believe and that much else in the New Testament is equally untrue. Consequently, huge numbers of Christian ministers stand up at Christmas and go through the motions, singing the carols and celebrating Christ's birth and Epiphany, all the time believing that it is no more than a delightful parable.[1]

If, however, Matthew's simple Magi story is rooted in the history, politics, and economics of Palestine and northern Arabia of the early first century, then the story is not a fabulous fiction after all. To be sure, it has been exaggerated and embroidered over the years, and it is true that this elaborate myth became the accepted version. But when we cut away all the accretions and rely only on Matthew's text and the historical evidence, a story rooted in history stands out clearly.

This matters because history matters, and history matters because truth matters. If we dismiss the story of the Magi as so much myth-making, then we must also doubt the rest of the gospel stories and dismiss them as late-invented magical tales. But if the Magi story is rooted in history, then we must treat the rest of the gospel stories with a similar seriousness. We should accept that there may have been elaborations and exaggerations over time, but we should also accept that the essential stories of the gospels are rooted in historical events first recorded by eyewitnesses.

This matters because the events of the life, ministry, death, and resurrection of Jesus Christ are the most history-shattering events of all time. If the gospel is historical then it is true, and if it is true, then we must confront the reality of Jesus Christ. And if we encounter Jesus Christ as a historical figure, then we must also deal with the question of who he is and what he accomplished.

Anyone who is honest and serious enough to embark on that quest will be following in the footsteps of the wise men themselves, who set out from the comfort of their own country on a dangerous mission to find not only a neighboring princeling but also the one they believed was the Prince of Peace.

Epilogue

WHAT HAPPENS TO THE EPIPHANY?

This book has been concerned with the historical foundation for Matthew's story of the Magi, and although I am a Catholic priest, I deliberately avoided sermonizing about the Magi. For the last two thousand years, Christians have celebrated the coming of the Wise Men to the Christ child in the feast of the Epiphany. During this church service, pastors and priests of all traditions have drawn inspirational lessons about life and truths about Jesus Christ for the edification and instruction of their flocks.

The paintings, stained-glass windows, and Bible illustrations, along with Christmas plays, carols, and cards, have all maintained the charming, mostly mythical, version of the story. The preaching points relied on this version, and some concerned Christian believers have shied away from this book because they dislike how I have dismantled the traditional, beloved stories about the Magi. Others have been disappointed with the factual basis of my research, thinking that it has somehow pulled the plug on the inspirational aspects of the Christmas story.

Have I shot down the Christmas angels in full flight with a barrage of historical facts? Must the preachers abandon their inspirational thoughts because they no longer match the facts? It does not need to be so. Indeed, the facts of the story that I have compiled support and enhance the points that preachers might wish to make about the story. It's just that they do so from a different and expanded angle.

The elaborations of the story came from two sources: the preaching of the members of the early church and the fantastic tales concocted by the gnostic writers. The stories about a burning babe floating through the night sky, the miraculous swaddling clothes thrown on a Zoroastrian fire, or the Magi from the land of Shir who found the Cave of Treasures with the wisdom of Seth are wild, fabulous, and ridiculous. While these stories influenced the Western tradition, they have for the most part disappeared. The later traditions—naming the Wise Men and appointing them as young, middle-aged, and old and from the three racial groups—live on in the iconography and colorful narratives surrounding the Magi. These traditions can be appreciated but not taken seriously as having any foundation in fact.

The preaching points and theological lessons, however, have a different bearing on the story and came about a different way. Matthew does not say there were three Magi or that they were kings. The fathers of the church, however, concluded that there were three kings because they conflated the passages in the Psalms and the prophecies of Isaiah with Matthew's text. In Psalm 72 and Isaiah 60, it is prophesied that kings will come to the Messiah from three nations. These passages, along with the presence of three gifts, dictated the number of Magi and their royal status.

Further preaching points were elaborated to discover the deeper meaning to the Magi story, and it is interesting to see how these traditional preaching points still hold, even though the factual details my research has uncovered do not support the preaching points in exactly the way they have been portrayed over the years. There are three basic applications that are still appropriate, even though the factual discoveries shift our perspective on them.

The first is the question of the number and royal status of the Magi. While these points were drawn from the Old Testament readings and not from Matthew's gospel, it is intriguing to note that there were three major ethnic and historical influences that came together in the development of the Nabatean culture. The indigenous Arabian tribes combined with the Babylonian culture that conquered the area and the Jewish refugees from the destruction of Jerusalem in 586 B.C. When Isaiah speaks of "Midian, Ephah, and Sheba," these three kingdoms or tribes from Arabia can well stand for the three-cultural influence that came together in the Nabatean culture.

Were the Magi kings? Probably not. But if they were envoys from the court of Aretas IV, then they were on a royal mission, and the preaching point about three kings bowing down to the King of Kings still carries weight.

The second traditional preaching point concerns the star of Bethlehem. It is a favorite trope for preachers to tell us that we must all "look heavenward to gain guidance from above." We are told how "the light from heaven will guide us step by step on our journey." The preacher might wax more eloquent and remind us that our journey through this life is akin to a journey at night through a barren desert. If the Magi's journey along well-traveled roads was comparatively short and they were not guided every step of the way by a magical moving star, do all those inspiring points crash like a falling star?

I don't think so, because the metaphor of the journey, the desert and the star still apply. They did set out on a journey, and it was through the desert. Although they were astrologers, the Magi really did look to the heavens for guidance. Rather than destroying the preaching point, the facts invest it with more profound meaning. The Magi's whole world view and cosmology were predicated upon a belief that the "heavens declare the glory of God and the firmament shows his handiwork" (Psalm 19). They believed the whole of creation was an interlocking system and by studying one part you could discern the hand of God in another.

A final preaching point is that the Wise Men, as non-Jews, represent all the nations of the world coming to the Messiah. This point was driven home by the later tradition that the Magi came from Persia, Africa, and Asia. That they actually came from the Nabatean kingdom makes this point even more vividly. Although they came from Petra, their Babylonian, Jewish, and Arabian ancestry was cosmopolitan. Furthermore, with their trading activities the Nabateans were a conduit for commodities and people from across the ancient world—from Britain and Spain in the west to India and China in the east. Their cultural, linguistic, and religious influences were spiced with contacts in Africa to the south and up into Syria, Asia Minor, and Eastern Europe to the north. If any nation represented the whole world at the time of Christ's birth, it was certainly the Nabateans.

We can see, therefore, that the lessons Christian ministers have taken from the story are not mistaken. It is their job to inspire believers with the deeper meaning of the story, and the factual focus of *The Mystery of the Magi* does not negate those points but amplifies them.

Acknowledgments

The idea for *Mystery of the Magi* first appeared when Dr. Matthew Bunson asked me to write an article about the origins of the wise men for *Catholic Answers* magazine. I was aware of the opinions of the academics that the Magi story was either a fantasy, or that the Magi (if they existed) were Zoroastrian priests from Parthia.

I wondered, however, if there might be more than meets the eye, and I asked whether the Old Testament prophecies about the Magi might indicate their origin. Reading "dromedaries from Midian and Ephah, and from Sheba they will come" in Isaiah turned my attention to Arabia. A bit of research opened up the fascinating history of the Nabatean people and the exotic intrigue of the incense trade routes, and soon the rest of the story of this book tumbled together in an amazing way.

I am not a scholar by any stretch of the imagination, so I am grateful for the courteous manner in which my questions were answered by those who are. Dr. David Graf, Dr. David Healey, and Dr. Judith McKenzie all helped with detailed information about the Nabateans. Professors Owen Gingrich and Michael Molnar clarified some points about the star, while Juan Antonio Belmonte helped me understand the archaeoastronomical aspects of Petra. Professor Andrea Polcaro very kindly took time during one of my visits to Italy to meet and discuss the basics of archaeoastronomy.

Professor Sir Colin Humphreys spent an extraordinary amount of time reading the manuscript of this book and offering detailed insights—especially on the Bethlehem star. It was a delight to meet Dr. Margaret Barker and receive her enthusiasm about the Nabatean wise men. New Testament scholars Dr. Brant Pitre and Dr. Scott Hahn encouraged the book, and Dr. Edwin Yamauchi kindly read the manuscript and offered extra information and insights.

Thanks also go to an excellent editor, Tom Spence, the Regnery team, Chris Pelicano for producing the maps, and Cale Stanley of Cornell University for the use of his diagrams of the temple at Khirbet et-Tannur. Thanks to Daniel Natal for his video work and help with permissions and images. Thanks also to the abbot and monks of Belmont who welcomed me for an extended retreat for research in the college library.

Gratitude must be expressed to my friends Sid Tate and Richard and Ruth Ballard for being early readers of the manuscript. I also thank various friends for trying not to let their eyes glaze over as I enthused about Herodian politics, the history of frankincense, and the intrigues of Nabonidus the Odd.

Finally, I wish to thank my wife Alison and our children for being patient with the hours I spend with my nose stuck in books and my eyes glued to a flickering screen.

Bibliography

Adair, Aaron, *The Star of Bethlehem*: *A Skeptical View*. Fareham, England: Onus Books, 2013.

Albright, W. F. and C. F. Mann. *Matthew, The Anchor Bible*. New York: Doubleday, 1971.

Allen, Lindsay. *The Persian Empire*. London: British Museum Press, 2005.

Alpass, Peter John. *The Religious Life of the Nabateans*. Durham: Durham Theses Online, 2011.

Bailey, K. E. *Jesus through Middle Eastern Eyes*. London: SPCK, 2008.

Barker, Margaret. *Christmas, The Original Story*. London: SPCK, 2008.

———. *Temple Theology, An Introduction*. London: SPCK, 2004.

————. *King of the Jews, Temple Theology in John's Gospel*. London: SPCK, 2014.

Bartlett, J. R. *Edom and the Edomites*. Sheffield: Sheffield Academic Press, 1989.

Bauckham, Richard. *Jesus and the Eyewitnesses: The Gospels as Eyewitness Testimony*. Grand Rapids: Eerdmans, 2008.

Bausani, Alessandro. *The Persians*. New York: St. Martin's Press, 1962.

Beaulieu, Paul-Alain. *The Reign of Nabodinus*. New Haven: Yale University Press, 1989.

————. "Nabonidus the Mad King: A Reconsideration of his Steles from Harran and Babylon." In *Representations of Political Power, Case Histories from Times of Change and Dissolving Order in the Ancient Mid East*, edited by Marlies Heinz and Marian H. Feldman. Winona Lake, IN: Eisenbrauns, 2007.

BeDuhn, Jason and Paul Allan Mirecki. *Frontiers of Faith: The Christian Encounter with Manichaeism in the Acts of Archelaus*. Boston: Brill, 2007.

Belmonte, Juan Antonio. *Light and Shadows over Petra: Astronomy and Landscape in Nabatean Lands*. Nexus Network Journal, 2013.

Black, David. *Why Four Gospels?* Cantonment: Energion Publications, 2012.

Black, Matthew, ed. *Peake's Commentary on the Bible*. London: Nelson, 1977.

Borg, M. and D. Crossan. *The First Christmas: What the Gospel Really Teach About Jesus's Birth*. San Francisco: HarperOne, 2007.

Bourbon, Fabio. *Petra, Jordan's Extraordinary Ancient City*. New York: Barnes and Noble Books, 2014.

Boyce, Mary. *Zoroastrians: Their Religious Beliefs and Practices*. New York: Routledge, 2001.

Briant, Pierre. *From Cyrus to Alexander, A History of the Persian Empire*. Winona Lake, IN: Eisenbrauns, 2002.

Briggs, C. W. *The Apostle Paul in Arabia* in The Biblical World, vol. 41, no. 4 (April 1913), Chicago, University of Chicago Press, 255–59.

Brock, Sebastian. "Christians in the Sassanian Empire: A Case of Divided Loyalties." In *Religion and National Identity (Studies in Church History, 18)*, edited by Stuart Mews. Oxford: Blackwell, 1982.

Brown, R. E. *The Birth of the Messiah: A Commentary on the Infancy Narratives in the Gospels of Matthew and Luke*. 2nd ed. New York: Doubleday, 1993.

Browning, Iain. *Petra*. Partridge, NJ: Noyes Press, 1973.

Burke, Tony and Brent Landau. *New Testament Apocrypha, vol. 1: More Noncanonical Scriptures*, Grand Rapids: Eerdmans, 2016.

Burton, Richard. *The Gold Mines of Midan*. London: C. Kegan Paul, 1878.

Cameron, Ron. *The Other Gospels*. Louisville: Westminster John Knox Press, 1982.

Castellano, Daniel J. *The Synoptic Problem, vol. 1: The Priority of St. Matthew's Gospel*, http:/www.arcaneknowledge.org/catholic/matthew.htm.

Colledge, Malcolm. *The Parthians*. New York: Frederick A. Praeger, 1967.

Collins, Robert. *The Medes and Persians*. New York: McGraw-Hill, 1972.

Corbett, Glenn. *The Edomite Stronghold of Sela*. Biblical Archeology Society, http://www.biblicalarchaeology.org/daily/biblical-sites-places/biblical-archaeology-sites/the-edomite-stronghold-of-sela/.

Dalley, Stephanie. *The Legacy of Mesopotamia*. Oxford: Oxford University Press, 2006.

Daniélou, Jean. *Primitive Christian Symbols*. London: Burns & Oates, 1964.

Dean, G. Davis, Jr. *Tithes and Offerings: Perspectives on Christian Giving*. Pittsburgh: Rose Dog Books, 2014.

Dougherty, Raymond P. *Nabonidus in Arabia*. Journal of the American Oriental Society, vol. 42 (1922).

Drower, E. S. *Mandaeans of Iran and Iraq*. Piscataway, NJ: Gorgias Press, 2002.

Eastburn, Gerardo. *The Esoteric Codex: Zoroastrianism*. www.lulu.com, 2015.

Eddy, Samuel K. *The King is Dead: Studies in Near Eastern Resistance to Hellenism, 334–31 BC*. Lincoln, NE: University of Nebraska Press, 1961.

Edwards, James. *The Hebrew Gospel and the Development of the Synoptic Tradition*. Grand Rapids: Eerdmans, 2009.

Eph'al, Israel. *The Ancient Arabs: Nomads on the Borders of the Fertile Crescent 9th–5th Centuries B.C.* Jerusalem: Magnes Press/ Leiden: Brill, 1982.

Evans, Tyler. *The Nabonidus Controversy*. Essay at www.academia.edu, http://www.academia.edu/26092587/The_Nabonidus_Controversy_Essay.

Finkelstein, Israel and Neil Asher Silberman. *David and Solomon: In Search of the Bible's Sacred Kings and the Roots of the Western Tradition*. New York: Free Press, 2007.

Flusser, David. *Jesus*. Jerusalem: Magnes Press, 2001.

Gadd, C. J. 1958. "The Harran Inscriptions of Nabonidus." *Anatolian Studies* 8: 35–92.

Gaetz, Heinrich. *History of the Jews, v.iii*. New York: Cosimo Books, 2009.

Gilbert, Martin. *The Routledge Atlas of Jewish History*. London: Psychology Press, 2003.

Gingrich, Owen. *God's Universe*. Cambridge, MA: Belknap Press of Harvard University Press, 2006.

Glueck, Nelson. *Deities and Dolphins*. New York: Farrar, Straus and Giroux, 1965.

Graf, David. *Rome and the Arabian Frontier: from the Nabateans to the Saracens*. Brookfield, VT: Ashgate, 1997.

———."Nabateans." In *The Anchor Bible Dictionary*, edited by David Freedman. New York: Doubleday, 1992.

Guillaume, Alfred. "The Arabic Background of the Book of Job." In *Promise and Fulfillment: Essays Presented to Professor S. H. Hooke*, edited by F. F. Bruce. Edinburgh: T&T Clark, 1963.

Hammond, Philip C. *The Temple of the Winged Lions*. Fountain Hills, AZ: Petra Publishing, 1996.

Hart, David Bentley. *Atheist Delusions*. New Haven: Yale University Press, 2009.

Haughton, Brian. *Hidden History*. Franklin Lakes, NJ: New Page Books, 2007.

Healey, John. *The Religion of the Nabateans: A Conspectus*. Boston: Brill, 2001.

Hendriksen, William. *Exposition of the Gospel According to Matthew*. Grand Rapids: Baker Book House, 1973.

Hitti, Philip K. *History of the Arabs*, 10th ed. London: MacMillan, 1970.

Hughes, David. *The Star of Bethlehem Mystery*. London: J. M. Dent, 1979.

Humphreys, Colin. *The Miracles of Exodus: A Scientist's Discovery of the Extraordinary Natural Causes of the Biblical Stories*. San Francisco: HarperOne, 2004.

———. *Star of Bethlehem, Comet in 5 BC*. Tyndale Bulletin, 42–44, "Ancient and Medieval Observations." no. 63.

Hunger, H. and D. E. Pingree. 1999. "Astral Sciences in Mesopotamia." In *Handbuch der Orientalistik, Erste Abteilung, Der Nahe Und Der Mittlere Osten*. Boston: Brill.

Hultgård, Anders. "The Magi and the Star—the Persian Background in Texts and Iconography." In *"Being Religious and Living through the Eyes": Studies in Religious Iconography and Iconology*, edited by Peter Schalk. Acta Universitatis Upsaliensis: Historia Religionum, 14. Uppsala, Almqvist & Wiksell International, 1998.

Hutchinson, Robert J. *Searching for Jesus*. Nashville: Thomas Nelson, 2015.

Johnston, Sarah I. *Religions of the Ancient World: A Guide*. Cambridge, MA: Belknap Press, 2004.

Kasher, Aryeh. *Jews, Idumeans and Ancient Arabs: Relations of the Jews in Eretz-Israel*. Tubingen: J. C. Mohr, 1988.

Key, Andrew F. *Traces of the Worship of the Moon God Sîn among the Early Israelites, The Journal of Biblical Literature*, vol. 84, no. 1, (March 1965) 20–26.

Kidger, Mark. *The Star of Bethlehem, An Astronomer's View.* Princeton: Princeton University Press, 1999.

Lambert, W. G. "The Historical Development of the Mesopotamian Pantheon: A Study in Sophisticated Polytheism." In *Unity and Diversity*, edited by Hans Goedicke. Baltimore/London: John Hopkins University Press, 1975.

Landau, Brent. *Revelation of the Magi: The Lost Tale of the Wise Men's Journey to Bethlehem.* New York: Harper Collins, 2010.

Leaf, Murray J. *The Anthropology of Western Religions: Ideas, Organizations and Constituencies.* New York: Lexington Books, 2014.

Leiva-Merikakis, Erasmo. *Fire of Mercy, Heart of the Word: Meditations on the Gospel According to St. Matthew.* San Francisco: Ignatius Press, 1996.

Lemaire, André. "Nabonidus in Arabia and Judah in the Neo Babylonian Period." In *Judah and the Judeans in the Neo Babylonian Period*, edited by Oded Lipschitz and Joseph Blenkinsopp. Winona Lake, IN: Eisenbrauns, 2003.

Losch, Richard. *The Uttermost Parts of the Earth: A Guide to Places in the Bible.* Grand Rapids: Eerdmans, 2005.

Maalouf, Tony. *Arabs in the Shadow of Israel.* Grand Rapids: Kregel Publications, 2003.

Macdonald, M. C. A. *Trade Routes and Trade Goods at the Northern End of the "Incense Road" in the First Millennium B.C.* No. IX in M. C. A. Macdonald. *Literacy and Identity in Pre-Islamic Arabia* (Variorum Collected Studies, 906). Farnham: Ashgate, 2009.

Marshak, Adam Kolman. *The Many Faces of Herod the Great.* Grand Rapids: Eerdmans, 2015.

Martin, Ernest. *The Star of Bethlehem, the Star that Astonished the World.* Portland, OR: Associates for Scriptural Knowledge, 1996.

McKenzie, Judith. *The Nabatean Temple at Khirbet et-Tannur.* Boston: American School of Oriental Research, 2013.

Mettinger, Tryggve N.D. *No Graven Image? Israelite Aniconism in Its Ancient Near Eastern Context.* Stockholm: Almvqvist & Wiksell, 1995.

Millar, Fergus. *The Roman Near East, 31 BC–AD 337.* Cambridge: Harvard University Press, 1993.

Millard, Alan R. "Daniel in Babylon: An Accurate Record?" In *Do Historical Matters Matter to Faith: A Critical Appraisal of Modern and Postmodern Approaches to Scripture*, edited by James K. Hoffmeier and Dennis R. Magary. Wheaton: Crossway, 2012.

Molnar, Michael. *The Star of Bethlehem, The Legacy of the Magi*. New Brunswick: Rutgers University Press, 1999.

Montgomery, James. *Arabia and the Bible*. Philadelphia: University of Pennsylvania Press, 1934.

Moore, Patrick. *The Star of Bethlehem*. Bath, England: Canopus, 2001.

Murphy O'Connor, Jerome. *The Essenes in Palestine*. The Biblical Archaeologist, vol. 40, no. 3 (September, 1977): 100–124.

Nersessian, Vrej. *The Bible in the Armenian Tradition*. Los Angeles: Getty, 2001.

Neubauer, A. "Where Are the Ten Tribes?" *Jewish Quarterly Review* 1. University of Michigan Library, 1966.

Nicholl, Colin. *The Great Christ Comet*. Wheaton: Crossway, 2015.

Nielsen, Kjeld. *Incense in Ancient Israel*. Leiden: Brill, 1986.

Parker, S. Thomas. *The Roman Frontier in Central Jordan: Final Report on the Limes Arabicus Project, 1980–1989*. Dumbarton Oaks: Dumbarton Oaks Research Library and Collection, 2006.

Parpola, Simo. "The Magi and the Star: Babylonian Astrology Dates Jesus' Birth." In *The First Christmas: The Story of Jesus' Birth in History and Tradition*, edited by Sara Murphy. Washington, DC: Biblical Archeology Society, 2009.

Patrich, Joseph. *Prohibition of Graven Images Among the Nabateans-the Testimony of the Masseboth Cult*. Cathedra, XXVI, 1982: 47–104.

Pitre, Brant. *The Case for Jesus*. New York: Image Books, 2016.

Ratzinger, Joseph. *The Infancy Narratives of Jesus of Nazareth*. New York: Random House, 2012.

Rawlinson, George. *The Story of the Nations: Parthia*. New York: G. P. Putnam, 1903.

Richardson, Peter. *Herod: King of the Jews and Friend of the Romans*. Columbia, SC: University of South Carolina Press, 1996.

Riesner, Rainer. *Paul's Early Period, Chronology, Mission Strategy, Theology.* Grand Rapids: Eerdmans, 1998.

Roberts, Courtney. *The Star of the Magi, The Mystery that Heralded the Coming of Christ.* Franklin Lake, NJ: New Page Books, 2007.

Roberts, Paul William. *In Search of the Birth of Jesus.* New York: Riverhead Books, 1995.

Sack, Ronald H. "The Nabonidus Legend." *Revue d'Assyriologie et d'archéologie orientale*, vol. 77, no. 1 (1983): 59–67.

Sanders, E. P. *The Historical Figure of Jesus.* London: Penguin, 1993.

Sandmel, Samuel. *Herod: Profile of a Tyrant.* Philadelphia/New York: Lippincott, 1967.

Saward, John. *Cradle of Redeeming Love.* San Francisco: Ignatius, 2002.

Schneemelcher, Wilhelm. *New Testament Apocrypha*, vol. 1. Louisville: Westminster John Knox Press, 1991.

Skarsaune, Oskar. *The Proof from Prophecy: A Study in Justin Martyr's Proof Text Tradition.* The Netherlands: Brill, 1987.

Stanton, Graham. *Jesus and Gospel.* Cambridge: Cambridge University Press, 2004.

Starcky, Jean. "The Nabateans: A Historical Sketch," *The Biblical Archaeologist*, vol. 18, no. 4: 81–82 and 84–106. Boston: The American Schools of Oriental Research, 1955.

Stearns, Peter N. and William Leonard Langer. *The Encyclopedia of World History.* 6th, illustrated ed. Boston: Houghton Mifflin Harcourt, 2001.

Sutcliffe, Edmund. *The Monks of Qumran.* Westminster, MD: The Newman Press, 1960.

Taylor, Jane. *Petra and the Lost Kingdoms of the Nabateans.* London: Tauris & Co, 2012.

Trexler, Richard. *The Journey of the Magi: Meanings in History of a Christian Story.* Princeton: Princeton University Press, 1997.

Tschanz, David W. *The Nabateans: A Brief History of Petra and Madain Saleh.* Surrey, UK: Medina, 2012.

Turner, David. *Matthew.* Ada: Baker Books, 2008.

van Kooten, George and Peter Barthel, eds. *The Star of Bethlehem and the Magi, Interdisciplinary Perspectives from Experts on the Ancient Near East, The Greco-Roman World, and Modern Astronomy*. Boston: Brill, 2015.

von Balthasar, Hans Urs. Translated by John Saward, *The Scandal of the Incarnation, Irenaeus Against the Heresies*. San Francisco: Ignatius, 1981.

Watson, Wilfred G. E, trans. *The Dead Sea Scrolls Translated: The Qumran Texts in English*. Leiden: Brill, 1994.

Waxman, Myer. "The importance of Palestine for Jews of the Diaspora in Past and Present." *The Maccabean: A Magazine of Jewish Life and Letters*, vol. 23, no. 1 (1913).

Wenning, Robert. *The Betyls of Petra*, http://archiv.ub.uni-heidelberg.de/propylaeumdok/1836/1/Wenning_Petra_2001.pdf.

Williams, Frank, Jr., trans. *The Panarion of Ephphanius of Salamis*, Book I, Sections 1–46. Leiden: Brill, 1987.

Williamson, H. G. M. *Variations on a Theme: King Messiah and Servant in the Book of Isaiah*. Milton Keynes: Paternoster, 2000.

Yamauchi, Edwin. "The Episode of the Magi." In *Chronos, Kairos, Christos, Nativity and Chronological Studies Presented to Jack Finigan*, edited by Jerry Vardaman and Edwin Yamauchi. Winona Lake: Eisenbrauns, 1989.

Yogananda, Paramahansa. *The Second Coming of Christ: The Resurrection of the Christ Within You*. Los Angeles: Self Realization Fellowship Publishers, 2004.

Notes

INTRODUCTION

1. Matthew 2:1–12, New International Version.

2. R. E. Brown, *The Birth of the Messiah* (New York: Doubleday, 1993), 6.

3. Ron Cameron, *The Other Gospels* (Louisville: Westminster John Knox Press, 1982), 109.

CHAPTER ONE

1. Robert J. Hutchinson has an excellent summary of the quest for the historical Jesus in chapter two of his *Searching for Jesus* (Nashville: Thomas Nelson, 2015).

2. Margaret Barker, *Temple Theology, An Introduction* (London: SPCK, 2004), 2.

3.   Raymond Brown, *The Birth of the Messiah: A Commentary on the Infancy Narratives in the Gospels of Matthew and Luke,* 2nd ed. (New York: Doubleday, 1993), 30–31.

4.   Marcus J. Borg and John Dominic Crossian, *The First Christmas: What the Gospels Really Teach about Jesus's Birth* (San Francisco: HarperOne, 2007).

5.   Brown, 33–34.

6.   Brown, 184ff.

7.   Isaiah 60:5–6, New American Bible.

8.   Brown, 25–26.

9.   Erasmo Leiva-Merikakis, *Fire of Mercy, Heart of the Word: Meditations on the Gospel According to St. Matthew,* vol. 2 (San Francisco: Ignatius Press, 2003), 44.

CHAPTER TWO

1.   Irenaeus, *Adversus haereses,* Book 3.

2.   Eusebius, *Ecclesiastical History,* Book 3, chapter 39, verse 16.

3.   David Turner, *Matthew* (Grand Rapids, MI: Baker Academic, 2008), 15–16.

4.   Daniel J. Castellano, *The Synoptic Problem,* vol. 1, http://www.arcaneknowledge.org/catholic/matthew.htm.

5.   For that matter, no one disagreed with this ancient tradition until the eighteenth century.

6.   Wilhelm Schneemelcher, *New Testament Apocrypha,* vol. 1 (Louisville: Westminster John Knox Press, 1991), 134–78.

7.   James Edwards, *The Hebrew Gospel and the Development of the Synoptic Tradition* (Grand Rapids, MI: Eerdmans, 2009).

8.   Brown, 188.

9.   1 Peter 5:13.

10.   Colossians 4:10, 2 Timothy 4:11, Philemon 23.

11.   Clement of Rome, Ignatius of Antioch, Tertullian, Irenaeus, and others recount the deaths of Peter and Paul in Rome.

12.   12 John 21:18–19.

13.   Acts 1:1.

14. For a good summary of the dating of the gospels, see chapter seven of Brant Pitre, *The Case for Jesus* (New York: Image, 2016).

15. David Alan Black, *Why Four Gospels? The Historical Origins of the Gospels*, 2nd ed. (Cantonment, Fla.: Energion Publications, 2010), 6–7.

16. A full discussion of the dating of the gospels can be found in Robert J. Hutchinson, *Searching for Jesus* (Nashville: Nelson Books, 2015), 27–38.

17. Mark D. Roberts, quoted in Hutchinson, *Searching for Jesus*, 32.

18. Hutchinson, 37.

19. For a more in-depth discussion of the historicity of Matthew's gospel, see chapter two of Colin Nicholl, *The Great Christ Comet: Revealing the True Star of Bethlehem* (Wheaton, IL: Crossway, 2015).

20. See the work of James M. Arlandson and Alan Millard explained in Hutchinson, *Searching for Jesus*, 33. See also chapter seven of Pitre, *The Case for Jesus*, in which he explains that in the religious culture of first-century Palestine, a rabbi's disciples would have diligently recorded their master's actions and teachings.

21. Acts 10.

22. Brown, 25–26.

23. The earliest fathers of the Church who write about the Magi story seem embarrassed that they were pagan magicians. Ignatius of Antioch and Justin Martyr (*circa* 100–*circa* 165) take the trouble to explain how, in coming to Bethlehem, the "evil" magic in the world was overthrown and superstition was replaced by the true light of Christ. Ignatius, *Epistle to the Ephesians*, xix.3; Justin Martyr, *Dialogue*, lxxvii.9.

CHAPTER THREE

1. An excellent explanation of the formation of the New Testament canon can be found at http://www.churchhistory101.com/docs/New-Testament-Canon.pdf.

2. The Protoevangelium of James can be read online at http://gnosis.org/library/gosjames.htm.

3. Ignatius of Antioch, *Epistle to the Ephesians*, chapter 19. In writing about the supreme brightness of the star, Ignatius seems to know the

Protoevangelium—evidence, perhaps, that it predates his death in AD 108 and is thus far older than most scholars think.

4. Richard Trexler, *The Journey of the Magi: Meanings in History of a Christian Story* (Princeton: Princeton University Press, 2014), 12.

5. Katharina Heyden, "The Legend of Aphroditianus," in Tony Burke and Brent Landau, eds., *New Testament Apocrypha: More Noncanonical Scriptures*, vol. 1 (Grand Rapids, MI: Eerdmans, 2016), 1–8.

6. Brown, 168–69.

7. Translated by Alexander Walker. *Ante-Nicene Fathers*, vol. 8, edited by Alexander Roberts, James Donaldson, and A. Cleveland Coxe (Buffalo, NY: Christian Literature Publishing Co., 1886), reproduced at http://www.newadvent.org/fathers/0806.htm.

8. Jason BeDuhn and Paul Mirecki, eds., *Frontiers of Faith: The Christian Encounter with Manichaeism in the Acts of Archelaus* (Leiden: Brill, 2007), 6–8.

9. Brent Landau, *Revelation of the Magi: The Lost Tale of the Wise Men's Journey to Bethlehem* (New York: HarperOne, 2010), 121.

10. Ibid., 121–22.

11. Colossians 2:8.

12. 1 Timothy 6:20–21.

13. 1 John 4:2–3.

14. 1 Corinthians 15:17.

15. 1 Corinthians 15:3–5.

16. *Excerpta Latina Barbari*, 51b, available at http://www.attalus.org/translate/barbari.html.

17. Brown, 198.

18. Witold Witakowski, "The Magi in Syriac Tradition," in George A. Kiraz, ed., *Malphono w-Rabo d-Malphone: Studies in Honor of Sebastian P. Brock* (Piscataway, NJ: Gorgias Press, 2008), 809–44.

19. Margaret Barker, *Christmas: The Original Story* (London: SPCK, 2008), 116.

20. http://www.hymnsandcarolsofchristmas.com/Text/concerning_the_magi_and_their_na.htm.

21. Trexler, 38.

22. Trexler, 39.

23. Quoted in Paul William Roberts, *In Search of the Birth of Jesus* (New York: Riverhead Books, 1995), 106.

24. Numbers 24:17.

25. Trexler, 3–8.

CHAPTER FOUR

1. Herodotus, *The Histories*, Book 1.101.

2. Brian Haughton, *Hidden History* (Franklin Lakes, NJ: New Page Books), 217–18.

3. Tacitus, *Annals*, 2.27; 12.22, 59; Pliny, *Natural History*, trans. H. Packham, Loeb Classical Library (Cambridge, MA: Harvard University Press, 1968–1969), 30.2.

4. Pierre Briant, *From Cyrus to Alexander: A History of the Persian Empire* (Winona Lake, IN: Eisenbrauns, 2002), 268.

5. John Saward, *Cradle of Redeeming Love*, (San Francisco: Ignatius, 2002), 338.

6. Briant, 266–68.

7. Courtney Roberts, *The Star of the Magi: The Mystery that Heralded the Coming of Christ*, (Franklin Lake, NJ: New Page Books, 2007), 52.

8. Gerardo Eastburn, *The Esoteric Codex: Zoroastrianism*, (lulu.com, 2015), 1–2.

9. Roberts, 69–70.

10. Haughton, 217–18.

11. Roberts, 60.

12. Briant, 96.

13. G. Dean Davis Jr., *Tithes and Offerings: Perspectives on Christian Giving* (Pittsburgh: Rose Dog Books, 2014), 83.

14. Dean, 83.

15. Ibid., 79.

16. Robert Collins, *The Medes and Persians: Conquerors and Diplomats* (New York: McGraw-Hill, 1975), 70.

17.   Sarah I. Johnston, ed., *Religions of the Ancient World: A Guide* (Cambridge, MA: Harvard University Press, 2004), 555.

18.   Samuel K. Eddy, *The King is Dead: Studies in Near Eastern Resistance to Hellenism, 334–31 B.C.* (Lincoln: University of Nebraska Press, 1961), 65.

19.   Roberts, 58.

20.   Eddy, 69.

21.   Paul William Roberts, *In Search of the Birth of Jesus: The Real Journey of the Magi* (New York: Riverhead Books, 1995), 355.

22.   Dean, 87.

23.   Eddy, 82.

24.   Ibid., 83.

25.   Quoted in Eddy, 83.

26.   Ibid., 91.

27.   George Rawlinson, *The Story of the Nations: Parthia* (New York: Putnam, 1903), 78.

28.   Dean, 88.

29.   Dean, 87–88.

30.   Rawlinson, 396.

31.   Ibid., 221–22.

32.   George van Kooten and Peter Barthel, eds., *The Star of Bethlehem and the Magi: Interdisciplinary Perspectives from Experts on the Ancient Near East, the Greco-Roman World, and Modern Astronomy* (Boston: Brill, 2015), 599.

CHAPTER FIVE

1.   John William Burgon, "Petra" (1845), http://www.poetryatlas.com/poetry/poem/3771/petra.html.

2.   David Graf, "Nabateans," in David Freedman, ed., *Anchor Bible Dictionary* (New York: Doubleday, 1992), 4:970.

3.   Diodorus Siculus, *The Library of History*, Book XIX, chapter 94, verses 6–9, (Cambridge, MA: Loeb Classical Library, vol. 10, 1954), 89–91.

4.   Jane Taylor, *Petra and the Lost Kingdoms of the Nabateans* (London: Tauris, 2001), 17.

5.   David W. Tschanz, *The Nabateans: A Brief History of Petra and Madain Saleh* (Surbiton, UK: Medina, 2012), 61.

6.   Ibid.

7.   Ibid., 64.

8.   Ibid., 65.

9.   Tony Maalouf, *Arabs in the Shadow of Israel* (Grand Rapids, MI: Kregel Publications, 2003), 171.

10.   Aryeh Kasher, *Jews, Idumaeans, and Ancient Arabs: Relations of the Jews in Eretz-Israel* (Tübingen: Mohr, 1988), 6.

11.   John F. Healey, *The Religion of the Nabateans: A Conspectus* (Boston: Brill, 2001), 25.

12.   S. Thomas Parker, *The Roman Frontier in Central Jordan: Final Report on the Limes Arabicus Project, 1980–1989* (Washington: Dumbarton Oaks Research Library and Collection, 2005), 525.

13.   The invasion of northern Arabia by Nebuchadnezzar is mentioned by the Old Testament prophet Jeremiah (Jeremiah 49:28–33), and the defeat of Edom, Moab, and the Ammonites is reported by the prophet Ezekiel (Ezekiel 25:8–14).

14.   Kasher, 2.

15.   David F. Graf, *Rome and the Arabian Frontier from the Nabateans to the Saracens* (Brookfield, VT: Ashgate, 1997), 59–60.

16.   Jean Starcky, "The Nabateans: A Historical Sketch," *Biblical Archaeologist*, vol. 18, no. 4 (1955), 87.

17.   J. R. Bartlett, *Edom and the Edomites* (Sheffield: Sheffield Academic Press, 1989), 173–74.

18.   Isaiah 60:7, Genesis 25:13, 1 Chronicles 1:29.

19.   Bartlett, 173.

20.   Ibid.

21.   Ibid., 174.

22.   Maalouf, 177.

23.   Philip C. Hammond, quoted in Tschanz, 168.

24.   Taylor, 17.

25.   Ibid., 17.

26.   Josephus, *The Jewish War*, I, Preface, paragraph 2.

27. Iain Browning, *Petra* (Partridge, NJ: Noyes Press, 1973), 29.

28. Adolf Neubauer, "Where Are the Ten Tribes?" *Jewish Quarterly Review*, vol. 1, 1888, 24.

29. Meyer Waxman, "The importance of Palestine for Jews of the Diaspora Past and Present," *The Maccabean: A Magazine of Jewish Life and Letters*, vol. 23, 234. Rabbi Waxman provides an exhaustive list of Jewish colonies dispersed across the ancient Middle East.

30. Heinrich Graetz, *History of the Jews*, vol. 3 (New York: Cosimo Books, 2009), 54.

31. Brown, 169.

32. Jacob Saphir, *Iben Safir* (vol. 1, chapter 43), Lyck 1866, 99a, in https://en.wikipedia.org/wiki/Yemenite_Jews.

33. Haggai Mazuz, "Massacre in Medina," Segula, vol. 3 (2010).

34. Margaret Barker, *Temple Theology: An Introduction* (London: SPCK, 2004), 8.

35. *Encyclopaedia Judaica* (2007), reproduced at http://www.encyclopedia.com/religion/encyclopedias-almanacs-transcripts-and-maps/tayma.

36. Genesis 25:15, 1 Chronicles 1:30.

37. Scholars believe the book of Job dates from the sixth century BC and its provenance is Arabia. Maalouf's extensive work in tracing the Arabian background of the book of Job and Old Testament wisdom literature is fascinating and compelling. Maalouf, chapters 6 and 7.

38. Maalouf, 189.

39. Margaret Barker, *Christmas: The Original Story* (London: SPCK, 2008), 121.

40. Barker has written extensively on the survival of Jewish first-temple theology and its influence on early Christianity.

41. The famous Nabatean temple at Khirbet et-Tannur resembles the Jewish tabernacle and temple in its floorplan.

42. Psalms 144:1. This webpage lists fifty-nine of the numerous Biblical reference to God as rock. http://bible.knowing-jesus.com/topics/God,-The-Rock.

43. John Healey, *The Religion of the Nabateans: A Conspectus* (Boston: Brill, 2001), 186ff.

44. Joseph Patrich, "Prohibition of Graven Images among the Nabateans: The Testimony of the Masseboth Cult," *Cathedra*, XXVI (1982), 47–104; cited in Kasher, 33.

45. Healey, 188.

46. Tryggve N. D. Mettinger, *No Graven Image? Israelite Aniconism in Its Ancient Near Eastern Context*, Coniectanea Biblica, Old Testament Series 42 (Stockholm: Almqvist & Wiksell, 1995), 58.

47. The Greek word *baetyl*, or *baetylos*, probably originated from the Punic *betel* or the Semitic *bethel*, both meaning the "house of God." http://www.forumancientcoins.com/moonmoth/baetyl_coins.html.

48. From private correspondence with Dr. Healey.

49. Margaret Barker, *Temple Theology, An Introduction*, (London: SPCK, 2004), 7.

50. Healey, 189–90.

CHAPTER SIX

1.   Kasher, 9.

2.   Nelson Glueck, *Deities and Dolphins: The Story of the Nabateans* (New York: Farrar, Straus & Giroux, 1965), 47–62.

3.   Philip C. Hammond, *The Temple of the Winged Lions* (Fountain Hills, AZ: Petra Publishing, 1996), 120.

4.   J. R. Bartlett, *Edom and the Edomites* (Sheffield: Sheffield Academic Press, 1989), 174.

5.   Kasher, 9.

6.   David Graf, *Rome and the Arabian Frontier: From the Nabateans to the Saracens* (Brookfield, VT: Ashgate, 1997), 63.

7.   Kasher, 19.

8.   Stephanie Dalley, "Occasions and Opportunities (i) To the Persian Conquest," *The Legacy of Mesopotamia*, Stephanie Dalley, ed. (Oxford: Oxford University Press, 1998), 30.

9.   Ibid.

10. Taylor, 33. The relief at Sela is virtually identical to a stele from Harran now in the British Museum.

11. The discovery of more information about King Nabonidus is another instance of archaeology's confirming the historicity of the Bible. For many years scholars thought Belshazzar, who is mentioned in the book of Daniel, was not the king, because there were no records of a King Belshazzar. The discovery of the Nabonidus Cylinders (clay cylinders, discovered at Harran in 1956, bearing cuneiform inscriptions from the mid-sixth century BC) showed that Belshazzar was the co-regent, ruling in Babylon on behalf of his father, Nabonidus, who was resident in Tayma.

12. The god Sin was first called En-zu. In the third millennium BC he was considered the Lord of Wisdom, Father of the Gods, and Chief of the Gods. See my later discussion in this chapter of Sin and monotheism.

13. André Lemaire, "Nabonidus in Arabia and Judah in the Neo Babylonian Period," *Judah and the Judeans in the Neo Babylonian Period*, Oded Lipschits and Joseph Blenkinsopp, eds. (Winona Lake, Ind.: Eisenbrauns, 2003), 287–88.

14. Browning, 32.

15. Tony Maalouf, *Arabs in the Shadow of Israel* (Grand Rapids, MI: Kregel Publications, 2003), 187–88.

16. A relief carving of Nabonidus similar to the one at Sela, also discovered at Tayma, confirms his influence there. http://www.andrewlawler.com/where-the-wells-never-go-dry/.

17. Ronald H. Sack, "The Nabonidus Legend," *Revue d'Assyriologie et d'archéologie orientale*, vol. 77, no. 1 (1983), 59–67, 64.

18. Graf, 49.

19. Raymond P. Dougherty, "Nabonidus in Arabia," *Journal of the American Oriental Society*, vol. 42 (1922), 309, 315.

20. Andrew Lawler, "Where the Wells Never Go Dry," http://www.andrewlawler.com/where-the-wells-never-go-dry/.

21. Alan R. Millard, "Daniel in Babylon: An Accurate Record?" in *Do Historical Matters Matter to Faith: A Critical Appraisal of Modern and Postmodern Approaches to Scripture*, James K. Hoffmeier and Dennis R. Magary, eds. (Wheaton, IL: Crossway, 2012), 269.

22. Martin Gilbert, *The Routledge Atlas of Jewish History* (London: Psychology Press, 2003), 28. See also Paul-Alain Beaulieu, *The Reign of Nabonidus* (New Haven: Yale University Press, 1989), 174. The recent discovery in Tayma of a grave stone from AD 203

inscribed with Jewish names confirms that the Jewish presence in Tayma continued well into the Nabatean period. Mohammed Al-Najem and M. C. A. Macdonald, "A New Nabatean Inscription from Tayma'," *Arabian Archaeology and Epigraphy*, 20 (2009), 208–17, https://www.academia.edu/4421344/A_new_ Nabatean_ inscription_from_Tayma._With_M._Al-Najem.

23. Murray J. Leaf, *The Anthropology of Western Religions: Ideas, Organizations, and Constituencies* (New York: Lexington Books, 2014), 67; C. J. Gadd, "The Harran Inscriptions of Nabonidus," *Anatolian Studies*, 8 (1958), 86.

24. John J. Collins, 4Q *Prayer of Nabonidus*, in Qumran Cave 4, XVII: Parabiblical Texts, Part 3, ed. James C. VanderKam (Oxford: Clarendon, 1996), 83–93; Florentino García Martinez, *The Dead Sea Scrolls Translated: The Qumran Texts in English*, trans. Wilfred G. E. Watson (Leiden: Brill, 1994), 289.

25. Alfred Guillaume, "The Arabic Background of the Book of Job," in *Promise and Fulfillment: Essays Presented to Professor S. H. Hooke*, F. F. Bruce, ed. (Edinburgh: T&T Clark, 1963), 106–127.

26. Lemaire, 286.

27. Colin Humphreys, *The Miracles of Exodus: A Scientist's Discovery of the Extraordinary Natural Causes of the Biblical Stories* (San Francisco: HarperOne, 2004), 300.

28. See note 12 above.

29. Tyler Evans, *The Nabonidus Controversy*, academia.edu, http://www.academia.edu/26092587/The_Nabonidus_Controversy_Essay, 2–3.

30. Genesis 11:31.

31. Genesis 25:15.

32. Andrew F. Key, "Traces of the Worship of the Moon God Sîn among the Early Israelites," *Journal of Biblical Literature*, vol. 84, no. 1 (March 1965), 20–26.

33. *Ancient Mesopotamian Gods and Goddesses*, http://oracc.museum.upenn.edu/amgg/listofdeities/nannasuen/.

34. Paul-Alain Beaulieu's suggestion that Nabodinus wanted to establish a unified religion for his whole empire is found in "Nabonidus the Mad King: A Reconsideration of his Steles from Harran and Babylon," *Representations of Political Power: Case Histories from Times of Change and Dissolving Order in the Ancient Near East*,

Marlies Heinz and Marian H Feldman, eds. (Winona Lake, IN: Eisenbrauns, 2007), 137–165.

35. Evans, 3.

36. Healy, 189–90.

37. Beaulieu, 163.

38. Herodotus, *Histories*, in Courtney Roberts, *The Star of the Magi: The Mystery that Heralded the Coming of Christ* (Franklin Lake, NJ: New Page Books, 2007), 83.

39. Lemaire, 286.

40. Quoted in Peter Barthel and George van Kooten, eds., *The Star of Bethlehem and the Magi: Interdisciplinary Perspectives from Experts on the Ancient Near East, the Greco-Roman World, and Modern Astronomy* (Boston: Brill, 2015), 503.

41. Tschanz, 133–38.

42. Glenn Corbett, *The Edomite Stronghold of Sela*, Biblical Archeology Society, http://www.biblicalarchaeology.org/daily/biblical-sites-places/biblical-archaeology-sites/the-edomite-stronghold-of-sela/.

43. "Ancient Mesopotamian Gods and Goddesses," http://oracc.museum.upenn.edu/amgg/listofdeities/nannasuen/.

44. Ibid.

45. Samuel K. Eddy, *The King is Dead: Studies in Near Eastern Resistance to Hellenism, 334–31 b.c.* (Lincoln: University of Nebraska Press, 1961), 65.

46. Roberts, 63.

47. Ibid.

48. Margaret Barker, *Christmas: The Original Story* (London: SPCK, 2008), 120.

49. Jean Daniélou, *Primitive Christian Symbols* (London: Burns & Oates, 1964), 115.

50. Michael Molnar, *The Star of Bethlehem: The Legacy of the Magi* (New Brunswick: Rutgers University Press, 1999), 40–41.

CHAPTER SEVEN

1.   See the discussion on approaches to prophecy in Brown, 146.

2.   K. Stendahl, "Matthew," Peake's Commentary on the Bible, Matthew Black, ed. (London: Nelson, 1977), 771.

3.   Ibid., 769.

4.   Augustine, *Quest. in Hept*, ii.73; PL 34:623.

5.   Hans Urs von Balthasar, *The Scandal of the Incarnation: Irenaeus Against the Heresies*, trans. John Saward (San Francisco: Ignatius, 1981), 64.

6.   There is an excellent discussion of Jesus' prophecies of the destruction of Jerusalem in chapter seven of Brant Pitre, *The Case for Jesus*.

7.   Ignatius of Antioch (d. AD 108) linked Balaam's prophecy to the Magi story, and the Jewish rebel leader Simon bar Kokhbar (d. AD 135) saw himself as the "star" in Balaam's prophecy.

8.   Brown, 190–96.

9.   Ibid., 195.

10.   Ibid., 168–69.

11.   Roberts, 155.

12.   Suetonius, *Life of Vespasian*, 4.5, and Tacitus, *Histories*, 5.13.

13.   Virgil, "The Eclogues of Virgil," in *Virgil's Works: The Aeneid, Eclogues, Georgics*, trans. J. W. Mackail (New York: Modern Library, 1934).

14.   Maalouf, chapter 6.

15.   Robert Kugler and Patrick Hartin, *An Introduction to the Bible* (Grand Rapids, MI: Eerdmans, 2009), 193.

16.   John Bright, "Isaiah," *Peake's Commentary on the Bible*, Matthew Black, ed. (London: Nelson, 1977), 489.

17.   Douglas Jones, "Isaiah II and III," *Peake's Commentary on the Bible*, 516.

18.   Lemaire, 286.

19.   The Dedanites were another northern Arabian nomadic tribe descended from Abraham mentioned in Genesis 10:7.

20.   Healey, 189–90.

21.   Kenneth E. Bailey, *Jesus through Middle Eastern Eyes: Cultural Studies in the Gospels* (Downers Grove, IL: IVP Academic, 2008), 54.

22. *Encyclopaedia Britannica*, "Saba," https://www.britannica.com/place/Saba-ancient-kingdom-Arabia.

23. Peter N. Stearns and William Leonard Langer, *Encyclopedia of World History*, 6th ed. (New York: Houghton Mifflin, 2001), 41.

24. This date is based on Carbon 14 dating; however, paleographic research suggests a date around the first century BC. See Georges Bonani, et. al., Radiocarbon, vol. 34, no. 3, 1992, 843–49, https://journals.uair.arizona.edu/index.php/radiocarbon/article/viewFile/1537/1541.

25. Courtney Roberts, *The Star of the Magi: The Mystery That Heralded the Coming of Christ* (Franklin Lake, NJ: New Page Books, 2007), 106.

26. Ibid.

CHAPTER EIGHT

1. Taylor, 30. Some scholars think the "rock" referred to is the hill fortress of Sela, not Petra.

2. Ibid., 33.

3. Tschanz, 20.

4. Ibid., 21.

5. Ibid.

6. Ibid., 22.

7. Kasher, 123–24.

8. Ibid., 131.

9. Maalouf, 191.

10. Kasher, 62.

11. Samuel Sandmel, *Herod: Profile of a Tyrant* (Philadelphia: Lippincott, 1967), 57–58.

12. Josephus, *The Jewish War*, I.6.2–4; I.8.9, in Maalouf, 190.

13. Kasher, 146.

14. Ibid., 138–39.

15. Ibid., 147–49.

16. Ibid., 152.

17. Ibid., 163.

18.   Ibid., 161–173.

19.   Ibid., 171.

20.   Ibid., 176.

CHAPTER NINE

1.   Brown, 199.

2.   "May the kings of Tarshish and the islands[d] bring tribute, the kings of Sheba and Seba offer gifts. May all kings bow before him, all nations serve him." Psalm 72:10–11.

3.   "So that they may bring you the wealth of nations, with their kings in the vanguard." Isaiah 60:11.

4.   Richard Losch, *The Uttermost Parts of the Earth: A Guide to Places in the Bible*, (Grand Rapids, MI: Eerdmans, 2005), 158.

5.   Brown, 543–44

6.   Ibid., 190.

7.   http://raregoldnuggets.com/blog/?p=1717.

8.   Philip K. Hitti, *History of the Arabs*, 10th ed. (London: Palgrave, 2002), 48.

9.   I Kings 10:10; Psalm 72; Isaiah 60:6; Ezekial 27:22; 38:13.

10.   Genesis 2:11 speaks of four rivers that flow from the Garden of Eden, the first of which is Pishon: "The name of the first is the Pishon; it is the one that winds through the whole land of Havilah, where there is gold."

11.   Richard Burton, *The Gold-Mines of Midian* (London: C. Kegan Paul, 1878).

12.   http://www.galaxie.com/article/bsp05-4-02.

13.   https://en.wikipedia.org/wiki/Mahd_adh_Dhahab.

14.   https://www.theguardian.com/science/2012/feb/12/archaeologists-and-quest-for-sheba-goldmines.

15.   Israel Finkelstein, Neil Asher Silberman, *David and Solomon: In Search of the Bible's Sacred Kings and the Roots of the Western Tradition*, (New York: Free Press, 2006), 171.

16.   Maalouf, 209.

17.   Psalm 141:2; Revelation 5:8; 8:3–4.

18. Exodus 30:1–8, 34–38

19. Jane Taylor, *Petra and the Lost Kingdoms of the Nabateans* (London: Tauris & Co, 2012), 19.

20. Ibid., 26.

21. Tschanz, 62.

22. Kjeld Nielsen, *Incense in Ancient Israel* (Leiden: Brill, 1986), 19.

23. Taylor, 22.

24. Herodotus, III.9, quoted in J. R. Bartlett, *Edom and the Edomites* (Sheffield: Sheffield Academic Press, 1989), 163.

25. Ibid., 10.

26. Ibid., 27.

27. Josephus, *Antiquities*, XVI, 1:136-41; quoted in Brown, 174.

28. Richard Trexler, *The Journey of the Magi: Meanings in History of a Christian Story*, (Princeton: Princeton University Press, 1997), 17.

29. Pierre Briant, *From Cyrus to Alexander, A History of the Persian Empire*, (Winona Lake, IN: Eisenbrauns, 2002), 68.

30. Maalouf, 160.

31. Ibid.

32. Ibid., 209.

33. Trexler, 17.

34. Psalm 72:10.

35. Trexler, 18.

36. Fergus Millar, *The Roman Near East, 31 BC–AD 337* (Cambridge: Harvard University Press, 1993), 40.

37. http://nabataea.net/horse.html.

38. Brown, 174.

39. This is the translation of the New American Bible.

CHAPTER TEN

1. Bradley E. Schaefer, "An Astronomical and Historical Evaluation of Molnar's Solution," in *The Star of Bethlehem and the Magi:*

Interdisciplinary Perspectives from Experts on the Ancient Near East, the Greco-Roman World, and Modern Astronomy, ed. George van Kooten and Peter Barthel (Boston: Brill, 2015), 85.

2.   Schaefer, 87.

3.   Ibid., 89.

4.   Patrick Moore, *The Star of Bethlehem* (Bath, England: Canopus, 2001), 72.

5.   Colin R. Nicholl, *The Great Christ Comet: Revealing the True Star of Bethlehem* (Wheaton, IL: Crossway, 2015), 80.

6.   Colin Humphreys, "The Star of Bethlehem," *Science and Christian Belief*, vol. 5, no. 2, (1993): 83–101.

7.   Courtney Roberts, *The Star of the Magi: The Mystery that Heralded the Coming of Christ* (Franklin Lakes, NJ: New Page Books, 2007), 90.

8.   Ibid., 105.

9.   Edwin Yamauchi, "The Episode of the Magi," in Jerry Vardaman and Edwin M. Yaumachi, eds., *Chronos, Kairos, Christos: Nativity and Chronological Studies Presented to Jack Finigan* (Winona Lake, IN: Eisenbrauns, 1989), 39.

10.   See Nicholl, 70–73, where he explains and debunks this theory.

11.   Michael Molnar, *The Star of Bethlehem: The Legacy of the Magi* (New Brunswick: Rutgers University Press, 1999).

12.   The carving of Nabonidus at the fort of Sela, for example, pictures him facing a star and crescent moon. See Fig. 7.

13.   Michael R. Molnar, *The Star of Bethlehem: The Legacy of the Magi* (New Brunswick: Rutgers University Press, 1999), 93–96.

14.   Ibid., 94.

15.   Ibid., 95.

16.   Ernest Martin, *The Star that Astonished the World* (Portland, OR: Associates for Scriptural Knowledge, 1996).

17.   https://gilgamesh42.wordpress.com/2013/02/13/the-star-of-bethlehem-documentary-a-critiical-view-index/.

18.   See the essays in Barthel and van Kooten. Nicholl also dismisses Molnar's theory, 74–76.

19.   Nicholl, 149.

20. Nicholl's comet would have been truly remarkable, and the failure of observers in the Middle East to see and record it while other comets were well known and recorded is a major problem.

21. See Mark Kidger, *The Star of Bethlehem: An Astronomer's View* (Princeton: Princeton University Press, 1999).

22. Humphreys, 101.

23. "Let your astrologers come forward, those stargazers who make predictions month by month, let them save you from what is coming upon you." Isaiah 47:13.

24. Andrew F. Key, "Traces of the Worship of the Moon God Sîn among the Early Israelites," *Journal of Biblical Literature*, vol. 84, no. 1 (March 1965), 20–26.

25. See Roberts, 105.

26. Roberts, 106.

27. Yamauchi, 35–38.

28. Ibid., 32–35.

29. Quoted in E. S. Drower, *The Mandaeans of Iran and Iraq: Their Cults, Customs, Magic Legends, and Folklore* (Leiden: Brill, 1962, originally published 1937), xvii.

30. Tschanz, 139.

31. Brown, 169.

32. Maalouf, 72.

33. Juan Antonio Belmonte, A. César González-García, and Andrea Polcaro, "Light and Shadows over Petra: Astronomy and Landscape in Nabatean Lands," *Nexus Network Journal*, vol. 15, no. 3 (December 2013), 487–501.

34. Belmonte, 487.

35. Confirming a shared culture with early Judaism, the layout of the temple at Khirbet et-Tannur echoes those of the Jewish tabernacle and the temple in Jerusalem.

36. Nelson Glueck, *Deities and Dolphins* (New York: Farrar, Straus and Giroux, 1965).

37. Glueck, 453.

38. Barthel and van Kooten, 298.

CHAPTER ELEVEN

1. Brent Landau, *Revelation of the Magi: The Lost Tale of the Wise Men's Journey to Bethlehem* (New York: HarperCollins, 2010), 7.

2. Vrej Nersessian, *The Bible in the Armenian Tradition* (Los Angeles: Getty Publications, 2001).

3. Otto von Freising, *Historia de duabus civitatibus*, 1146, in Friedrich Zarncke, Der Priester Johannes (Leipzig: Hirzel, 1879, reprinted Hildesheim/New York: Georg Olms Verlag, 1980), 848; from https://en.wikipedia.org/wiki/Biblical_Magi#cite_note-37.

4. http://www.gurdjieffdominican.com/time_of_christ_Bennett.htm.

5. Paramahansa Yogananda, *The Second Coming of Christ: The Resurrection of the Christ Within You* (Los Angeles: Self Realization Fellowship, 2004), 56–59.

6. Brown, 198.

7. Eusebius, *Church History* 3, 5.

8. Mathieu Ossendrijver, "The Story of the Magi in the Light of Alexander the Great's Encounters with Chaldeans," in *The Star of Bethlehem and the Magi: Interdisciplinary Perspectives from Experts on the Ancient Near East, The Greco-Roman World, and Modern Astronomy*, eds. George van Kooten and Peter Barthel (Boston: Brill, 2015), 225.

9. Brown, 167.

10. Maalouf, 197.

11. Ibid.

12. Roberts, 29.

13. Ibid., 52.

14. Molnar, 37.

15. Pliny, *Natural History*, 25, 12–13, quoted in Barthel and van Kooten, 225.

16. Roberts, 63.

17. Daniélou, 115.

18. Brown, 45.

19. Maalouf, 206–8.

20. Ibid., 207.

21. Ibid.

22.   Brown, 169; cf. 1 Kings 5:10, Proverbs 30:1 and 31:1.

23.   Maalouf, 206.

24.   Margaret Barker, *Christmas: The Original Story* (London: SPCK, 2008), 116. Barker refers to Mishnah *Gittim*, 1.2 and Josephus, *Antiquities*, 4.7.

25.   James Montgomery, *Arabia and the Bible* (Philadelphia: University of Pennsylvania Press, 1934), 56–57; quoted in Maalouf, 207.

26.   Maalouf, 332, n. 10.

27.   C. W. Briggs, "The Apostle Paul in Arabia," *The Biblical World*, vol. 41, no. 4 (April 1913), 257.

28.   Philip K. Hitti, *History of the Arabs*, 10th ed. (London: Macmillan, 1970), 43.

29.   Brown, 168.

30.   Justin Martyr, *Dialogue*, lxxxviii 1.

31.   Tertullian, *Adversus Marcion*, iii 13.

32.   Clement of Rome, *Letter to the Corinthians*, 25:1–2.

33.   Frank Williams, trans., *The Panarion of Ephphanius of Salamis*, Book I, Sections 1–46 (Leiden: Brill, 1987), 645.

34.   Maalouf, 200.

CHAPTER TWELVE

1.   Margaret Barker, *Christmas: The Original Story* (London: SPCK, 2008), 123. The fact that they were headed toward Arabia lends credence to their Nabatean origins.

2.   Ibid., 122.

3.   Jean Daniélou, *Primitive Christian Symbols* (London: Burns & Oates, 1964), 115–123.

4.   Tertullian, *Adversus Marcion*, iii, 13.

5.   Justin Martyr, *Dialogue with Trypho*, chapter 78.

6.   The history of the Essenes is hotly debated because the evidence is slim and often contradictory. Because of their secretive nature and their persecution, what evidence we have is cryptic.

7.   Jerome Murphy-O'Connor, "The Essenes in Palestine," *The Biblical Archaeologist*, vol. 40, no. 3 (September 1977), 100–124. Murphy-O'Connor goes so far as to suggest that the Essenes were Jews who

returned from exile in Babylon and that "Damascus" was a code word for Babylon. This seems a fragile speculation.

8.   Acts 8:1–3; Philippians 3:6.

9.   Daniélou, ibid., 119. Daniélou cites Adolf von Harnack, *The Mission and Expansion of Christianity in the First Three Centuries* (London: Williams and Norgate, 1908). The existence of an early Jewish-Essene-Christian community at Kokhba is also mentioned by Rainer Riesner in *Paul's Early Period: Chronology, Mission Strategy, Theology* (Grand Rapids, MI: Eerdmans, 1998) 239, especially note 24.

10. For a good overview of the theories about Paul's mysterious stay in Arabia, see Riesner, 256–60.

11. Briggs, 255–59.

12. Riesner, 260, note 133.

13. Barker, 120.

14. Ibid., 122.

15. Galatians 2:15–16 is just one example.

16. The thesis that early Christianity was derived from the mystery religions has been debunked. Instead we can see that Paul used some of the language and imagery from mystery religions to communicate the gospel of Jesus Christ to his Gentile audience. See Raymond E. Brown, *The Semitic Background of the Term "Mystery" in the New Testament* (Philadelphia: Fortress Press, 1968), F. F. Bruce, *Paul and Jesus* (Grand Rapids, MI: Baker, 1974), H. A. A. Kennedy, *St. Paul and the Mystery Religions* (New York: Hodder and Stoughton, 1913), et al.

17. This webpage lists twenty-six direct quotations or allusions to Greek philosophers in the writings of Paul: https://biblethings inbibleways.wordpress.com/2013/07/14/paul-and-his-use-of-greek-philosophy/.

18. 2 Corinthians 11:32. When Paul returned to Damascus after his stay in Arabia the governor of the city, under the instructions of Aretas IV, tried to detain him.

19. Daniélou, 122.

20. The heretical Simon the Magus was active in Samaria, and the Apostles had to counter his false teaching. Acts 8:9–21.

CONCLUSION

1.   This is the view of Marcus J. Borg and John Dominic Crossan in *The First Christmas: What the Gospels Really Teach about Jesus's Birth* (San Francisco: HarperOne, 2007).

Index